C000178165

IMAGES OF ENGLAND

CENTRAL
BIRMINGHAM
PUBS

BIRMINGHAM ALE TASTERS

(Tune: How happy a state does a miller possess)

Of all civil officers annually chose,
There's none in the kingdom are equal to those,
Whose duty requires, a little more to rove,
And taste at the pleasure, what ENGLISHMEN love.

From Bord'sly to Hockley our PROVINCE extends,
I wish we had time to address all our friends;
Of houses all free-cost, to visit, 'tis clear,
The number is more than are days in the year.

We carry no truncheons, our power to show,
With government matters have nothing to do;
We drink with the common, yet rank with the best,
And like ALDERMEN live at a LOW BAILIFF's FEAST.

Our good BROTHER OFFICERS strangers must be,
When beating our rounds, to the pleasure we see;
From office of CONSTABLE troubles ensue,
But that of a TASTER is joy year through.

For when upon duty, as custom has taught,
We call for a TANKARD, 'tis instantly brought;
And how pleasing it is for a Landlord to say,
'You're welcome, kind sir, - there is nothing to pay'.

We visit the MARKETS, and traverse the STREETS,
Our CHIEF to assist, in adjusting the weights;
And wish 'twere the practice, in all kinds of sales,
To down with the steelyards, and up with the scales.

The BUTCHERS may throw out their marrow-bone spite,
But reason informs us 'tis nothing but right;
For JUSTICE relying on TRUTH as her guide,
When pictur'd, has always the SCALES by her side.

Fill a bumper to TRADE, 'tis the TASTER'S request,
With plenty may BRITAIN for ever be blest;
Where discord abounds, may true friendship commence,
And BIRMINGHAM 'flourish a thousand years hence'.

JOHN FREETH
[1782]

IMAGES OF ENGLAND

CENTRAL BIRMINGHAM PUBS

JOSEPH MCKENNA

TEMPUS

First published 2006

Tempus Publishing Limited
The Mill, Brimscombe Port,
Stroud, Gloucestershire, GL5 2QG
www.tempus-publishing.com

© Joseph McKenna, 2006

The right of Joseph McKenna to be identified as the Author
of this work has been asserted in accordance with the
Copyrights, Designs and Patents Act 1988.

All rights reserved. No part of this book may be reprinted
or reproduced or utilised in any form or by any electronic,
mechanical or other means, now known or hereafter invented,
including photocopying and recording, or in any information
storage or retrieval system, without the permission in writing
from the Publishers.

British Library Cataloguing in Publication Data.
A catalogue record for this book is available from the British Library.

ISBN 0 7524 3873 5

Typesetting and origination by Tempus Publishing Limited.
Printed in Great Britain.

CONTENTS

ACKNOWLEDGEMENTS

My thanks to my former colleagues in the Central Library, Birmingham, who unknowingly in a series of pub crawls around central Birmingham during the 1980s and 1990s, were laying the groundwork for this study. My thanks also for the publicans who served us, and in particular Nancy and Paddy McCarthy of the Prince of Wales, in Cambridge Street, who's pub became a second home for many of us. Finally a note of gratitude to my wife Wendy, who came to realise that though I might return home tipsy, it was all in the interest of research.

INTRODUCTION

This is the second of a series of books on Birmingham pubs, published by Tempus. The first, Birmingham Pubs, was compiled by Keith Turner in 1999. It gave a general overview of the public houses of Birmingham and its suburbs. This second book looks in more detail at the social and historical function of the public house within the city. To do any justice to such a study, the city has been broken up into bite-size chunks. This second book records the pubs, inns, taverns and beerhouses that lie, and lay, within the present Inner Ring Road and the Bull Ring.

The public house as we know it, and in particular the inn, has its origins in the religious houses of pre-Reformation England. They would have supplied meals and beds to the traveller and pilgrim. Originally these 'hospitals' (from which we derive the word hospitality), were run by monks, but later these functions were delegated to trusted non-religious officials. By the sixteenth century deeds and surveys begin to give us the names of these publicans and their houses. Sketchley's Birmingham Directory of 1767 matches up publicans and their pubs. In the year of its publication there were 294 licensees listed. *Aris's Gazette*, the local newspaper, founded in 1741, puts flesh onto bones. Public houses had moved on from merely supplying food and drink to staging exhibitions, competitions, exchanges and auctions. Some houses had skittle and marble alleys, others had debating societies, reading societies, political, philosophical and educational reform societies. At the Golden Cross in Snow Hill was set up the world's first building society.

Stringent rules were drawn up by the magistrates respecting the issue of licenses. Applicants had to appear personally and show that they were persons of integrity, and give assurances that they would discourage tippling. Penalties were levied. An ale-house keeper encouraging tippling would be fined 10 shillings. One encouraging gaming on his premises could be fined 40 shillings for the first offence, and £10 for any subsequent offence. An ale-house keeper who was discovered to be drunk would forfeit his license for three years.

During the seventeenth century, Parliament encouraged the expansion of the gin trade, but this policy proved debilitating on the national fibre. The drinking of good wholesome English beer was encouraged once more. An Ale House Act was passed in 1828. This was followed by the Beer Act of 1830, which enabled any householder whose name was on the Rate Book to brew and sell beer, but no other intoxicating liquor, without having recourse to the local magistrates, merely by paying two guineas to the Excise. Within the first three months of the Act coming into force, nearly 25,000 licenses were issued nationwide. Public houses came under serious competition from these retail brewers who, with smaller overheads, could charge less for their beer. The publicans responded by enlarging their premises and increased the attraction of their houses by starting up societies and glee clubs, the fore-runners of the music hall. The big brewers meanwhile petitioned for reform. In an Act of 1869 the beerhouses were brought under magisterial control, like other licensed houses.

The late nineteenth century saw the rise of the brewery tied house. In order to sell their beer, breweries began to buy up public houses when they came onto the market. By 1890 the newly established Holt Brewery had 155 tied houses in and around the city. Ansells had sixty-four and Mitchell's had eighty-six. Gradually the free trade, the small independent publicans, were squeezed out. They simply could not afford to buy houses when they came up for sale by auction. In 1896 the Chairman of the Licensing Committee in Birmingham, Arthur Chamberlain, held a series of meetings with the brewers, with a view to showing how it would be possible for them to meet the wishes of the magistrates for the reduction in the number of licenses, without injuring their financial position. Smaller loss making houses were closed; the cost of rent, rates, taxes and repairs was recouped by the brewers. Owners of public houses that were closed by agreement, were paid compensation for their loss. What resulted was a monopoly situation, with two breweries, Ansells and M&B, owning virtually all the public houses in the city. This monopoly was further increased by a system worked out by the City Council in 1945, called 'barrelage', where public houses affected by war damage or future redevelopment should not suffer financially. Rather than pay compensation, the Licensing Planning Committee agreed that the brewers would keep barrelage. Unless a brewery had barrelage, resulting from the closure of a public house, the Licensing Committee would not give planning permission for the opening of a new pub. As Ansells and M&B had a virtual monopoly, the only way for a new brewer to get barrelage was to purchase it from them. This was usually reckoned to be 2,000 barrels, at £10 a barrel. Added to this, it was at the discretion of the big two as to whether they wished to sell or not. Thus the system was perpetuated, and choice to the public denied. However in a High Court ruling in December 1971, the system was declared illegal.

A report by the Monopolies Commission in the previous year, 1970, had criticised the fact that some breweries' pub ownership was too great in some areas. Birmingham was shown to be operating such a monopoly, and in the face of subsequent legislation, the great pub swap of 1978 took place. Robin Thompson, chief Executive of Ansells, cynically declared: 'We were told that the public demanded a wider choice of beer and now we are giving it to them.' Ansells swapped ninety pubs with Courage, rather than see them close under proposed Government legislation. Following further legislation in June 1990 to loosen the grip of the big brewers and encourage them to sell the products of smaller brewers in their pubs, an investigation by the Monopolies and Mergers Commission revealed that in Birmingham the scheme was being actively blocked by Ansells, who had hinted to their tenants that they would put up the rent of those selling other breweries' beers. Thus exposed, and warned, the brewers' next wheeze was the starting up of the Pubco. These companies, in the early days, were usually started up by former big brewery executives taking over pubs no longer required by the big brewers, with the financial assistance of those big brewers, and selling the produce of those self-same big brewers. Things are slowly improving, however, with the next generation of Pubcos, who genuinely seem to be offering a greater choice.

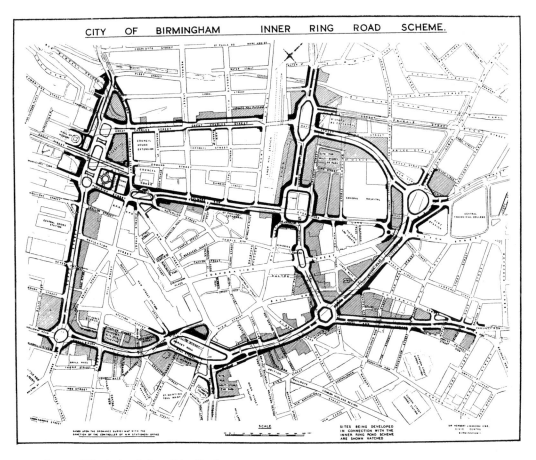

A map of Birmingham's Inner Ring Road.

Meanwhile, under pressure from the City Council, in April 1983 the Licensing Committee extended opening hours on Friday and Saturday nights from 10.30 to 11.00 p.m. Increasingly the Licensing Committee and its chairman, Mr Robert Price, were seen as hindering Birmingham's bid for recognition as an international city. In March 1990 matters came to a head. Price, who had been chairman of the Licensing Committee for twenty-two years, was publicly attacked by the NEC/ICC committee for imposing fifteen different conditions before granting a license for the National Indoor Arena. Both Conservative and Labour MPs complained to the Lord Chancellor about this abuse of power. In a secret ballot of the city's magistrates, Price failed to be re-elected to the Licensing Committee. A new forward committee, more in tune with the modern day requirements of the city, was elected. In 2003 Parliament passed a Licensing Act, which established a new system for regulating the sale of alcohol, public entertainment, late night refreshment and hot food takeaways. The Act switched the responsibility for issuing liquor licenses from magistrates' courts to the local authority. On 7 February 2005 the Act came into law.

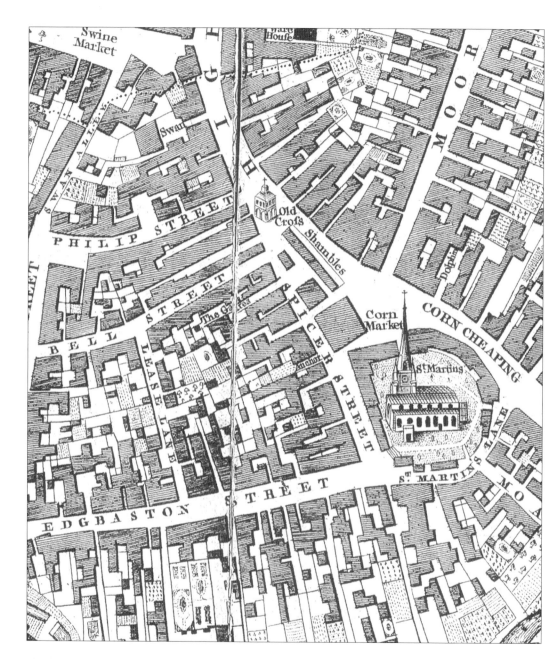

Map of the Bull Ring and its environs, 1750.

ONE

THE BULL RING PUBS

The Bull Ring is the very heart of Birmingham – here is situated its parish church and its original village. Its oldest inns were built around its market place, the earliest of which was the Red Lion. Its narrow frontage onto the street was but a burgage width, confirming its antiquity. This timber-framed inn was in existence by 1494. In that year 'Rico Mershall and Margaret' his wife leased the Red Lion from the Guild of St John the Baptist. In the 1552 Probate Inventory of Thomas Marshall, their grandson, it is revealed that at the time of his death he had 'two tuns of Gascony wine and one tun of sack [a Spanish wine]' in his cellars. The inn was immortalised in the Battle of Birmingham Tracts, being the scene of the brutal murder of Mr Whitehall, in 1643. In the Hearth Tax returns of 1663, John Hyatt is listed as landlord. Soon after the Red Lion was acquired by John Peake, a Governor of King Edward School. By 1680 the house was in the possession of the Milward family who leased it out to fund the Milward Charity, to help Birmingham's poor. Its landlord between 1710 and 1713 was Richard Shakle. By 1737, under landlord William Jordon, the Red Lion was known as a starting house for carrier wagons to all parts of the country. Birmingham's earliest known debating society, the Robin Hood, first met here in 1774.

In the late eighteenth century the front of the Red Lion was refaced in brick, and extensive renovation work was undertaken. However one timber-framed wall did survive. Charles Neville was licensee in the first decade of the nineteenth century. Edward Williams was licensee in 1816, and there is a short obituary notice for another licensee, Jonathan Welch, in May 1824. In the mid-nineteenth century, John Botterill, a former guard on the mail coach *Eclipse Tallyho*, and something of a local character, briefly ran the inn. A further refurbishment took place in 1885, following plans submitted on 10 September. The front was rebuilt in mock timber-framing, to a design that was to last until its closure in 1956. The Red Lion, then an Ansells house, was demolished to make room for a multi-storey car park for the Bull Ring Centre of the 1960s.

The Dolphin was an old timber-framed coaching inn, situated one door down from the Red Lion. It was probably sixteenth century in origin. In 1663, according to the Hearth Tax returns, its owner was John Brewerton. By 1676 it had been acquired by Nathaniel Pemberton. In the eighteenth century the house had become known as a coaching inn. The Birmingham and Warwick stagecoach for London, went from the Dolphin Inn on Mondays, Wednesdays and Fridays at 4.00 a.m. Passengers were charged £1 to travel inside, ten shillings outside. The

Left: *The Red Lion, Bull Ring, 1958.*

Below: *Red Lion, an interior view, 1949.*

Dolphin, marked on Samuel Bradford's Plan of Birmingham for 1750, was used as a meeting place to protest at the rise in duty on ale:

> The Publicans of this Town are desired to meet at the House of Mr Jordan, at the Dolphin in the Bull Ring, on Wednesday next, at Two o'clock in the Afternoon, to consult of a proper Method, to petition his Majesty for a Repeal of the late Act for the addition of Duty on Ale.
>
> (*Aris's Gazette*, 9 February 1761)

The Dolphin was demolished following the Birmingham Improvement Act of 1790, when a number of buildings in and around the Bull Ring were cleared with a view to creating a 'new and commodious market'.

There were three eighteenth-century public houses in the Bull Ring whose addresses have not been recorded; the Black Lion, the Lamb and the White Horse. The only record of the Black Lion is an advertisement in *Aris's Gazette* for 19 April 1762. The Lamb is recorded in Local Notes & Queries (1074). The site was given as the Bull Ring, but is 'not now traceable', the entry relates. The White Horse is safe to date as post-1715. The white horse was the coat of arms of the House of Hanover. There is an advertisement in the *Gazette* for 18 December 1797 informing the public that the White Lion was an ideal place for the trading of grain, being situated close to the corn and garden market, and thereby well accustomed.

At the northern end of the Bull Ring, near its junction with New Street, was situated the old coaching inn known as the Swan. It too was probably medieval in origin. The earliest dated reference to it appears in the Survey of Birmingham for 1553, which records that it was held by Robert Rastell. In 1560, Joan Ellyott married William Jennens, 'innholder' of the Swan. Over the next twenty-four years the couple had ten children. From this family was descended John Jennens, ironmaster, who became a millionaire. Not leaving a will, the family fortune was contested for a hundred years or so. Charles Dickens, a frequent visitor to the town, hearing of the case, featured it in Bleak House. For the story he changed the family name to Jarndyce. It was at this old inn during the Civil War that Thomas, the ostler at the Swan, was pistolled and killed by the Royalists. In 1663, according to the Hearth Tax returns, the landlord of the Swan was Philip Freher, a Governor of King Edward School. Two years later, as is shown in the rating returns, John Parttison was landlord. During the last decade of the century the Foxall family, who had made their fortune as iron merchants, acquired the Swan. Ambrose Foxall granted a lease of the inn to Edward Crank in 1707. In 1731, Nicholas Rothwell jr, whose father had initiated a Birmingham to London coach in 1691, operating from the Reindeer in High Street, transferred operations to the Swan.

John Barber was licensee in 1767. He was succeeded by Thomas Hart. The Foxall family, who still owned the house, sold it in 1780 to the Carver family, who also leased it out. Guests at the Swan included General Burgoyne, British Commander, General Elliott, the gallant defender of Gibraltar, Daniel O'Connell, the Irish Nationalist MP, and Charles Dickens, the author. With the establishment of the new Hen & Chickens in New Street, the Swan lost its status as the premier posting inn. It continued on throughout the century and into the next, a comfortable rather than luxurious house. The Swan was a casualty of the 1941 war-time Blitz.

Officially the Bull Ring is but a short stretch of road between Moor Street and Park Street. To many though it was that funnel-shaped area between the parish church and the junction of New Street and High Street, including Spiceal Street. Here was situated at 3-4 Spiceal

The Swan Hotel, High Street, early nineteenth century.

BIRMINGHAM STAGE-COACH,

In Two Days and a half; begins May the 24th, 1731.

SET out from the *Swan-Inn* in *Birmingham*, every *Monday* at fix a Clock in the Morning, through *Warwick*, *Banbury* and *Alesbury*, to the *Red Lion Inn* in *Alderfgate ftreet*, *London*, every *Wednefday* Morning: And returns from the faid *Red Lion Inn* every *Thurfday* Morning at five a Clock the fame Way to the *Swan-Inn* in *Birmingham* every *Saturday*, at 21 Shillings each Paffenger, and 18 Shillings from *Warwick*, who has liberty to carry 14 Pounds in Weight, and all above to pay *One Penny a Pound*.
Perform'd (if God permit)

By Nicholas Rothwell.

The Weekly Waggon fets out every *Tuefday* from the *Nagg's-Head* in *Bmiurgham*, to the *Red Lion Inn* aforefaid, every *Saturday*; and returns from the faid Inn every *Monday*, to the *Nagg's-Head* in *Birmingham* every *Thurfday*.

Note. By the faid Nicholas Rothwell at *Warwick*, all Perfons may be furnifhed with a *By-Coach*, *Chariot*, *Chaife*, or *Hearfe*, with a Mourning Coach and able *Horfes*, to any Part of *Great Britain*, at reafonable Rates: And alfo Saddle Horfes to be had.

The Birmingham to London stagecoach ran from the Swan in Birmingham.

Street another ancient inn. Its original name was the Maiden's Head, its inn sign depicting a painting of the Virgin Mary, patron of the Mercers' Company. The house is first referred to in a Guild Rental of 1524: 'Thomas Cowper heir to John Cowper butcher for his tenement in the Market place called the Maydenhead.'

In a deed of 1550 the house is described as the 'Meydenhedde nighe the high cross, tenanted by the above, "Thomas Couper"'. Following the Reformation the name of the house was changed to the Talbot, but because of its inn sign it was more popularly known as The Dog. The Talbots were Earls of Shrewsbury, who gave their name to a species of large white hunting dog, depicted on the board. By 1625 the house was in the keeping of the Lea family. On 1 January 1680 the inn was described as 'scituate or being in a certain street called Spicers Street, commonly called or known by the signe of the Talbot'. By then the building had been divided into two tenements, one of which was let in 1679 to 'Thomas Bird, saddler, for £3 10s per annum, and one fatt goose at Christmasse'. The tenancy of the inn itself passed from John Cooper to Jonathan Rowe, who paid £25 per annum, and in 1700 to Richard Halfpenny, whose annual rent was £34 10s. In 1709 the tenant was John Hargrave, in whose lease the inn was described as the Talbot alias the Dogg, in Spicers Street alias Mercers Street. It would appear that about this time the house was faced in brick. John Brown is listed in the trade directory of 1779 as its landlord, though the house is not named. He is referred to as innkeeper, 3-4 Spiceal Street. Richard Garnett was landlord from 1780 until his death on 28 July 1787, a fact recorded in Aris's Gazette two days later. His widow Margaret took up the license, but in September 1791 she sold the premises to Samuel Wyer. Very kindly she inserted the following advertisement in the Gazette:

DOG INN, Birmingham
M. Garnett respectfully returns her grateful Acknowledgments to
Her Friends and the Public in general, for the Favours received
During the Time of her occupying that House, and begs leave to
Recommend Mr Wyer as her Successor, for whom she particularly
Solicit's a Continuance of their favours.

After the death of Admiral Lord Nelson at Trafalgar in 1805, a statue was erected to the Admiral on the site of the old Market Cross, and the Dog Inn was renamed the Lord Nelson Inn. This old house, whose history dated back some 400 years, was demolished for the building of the Fish Market, which opened in 1869.

Also in Spiceal Street was the Woolpack, at No. 26. It was one of the smaller taverns in the Bull Ring. The date when it became a public house is unknown. William Poney was licensee from 1784 to 1801. During the period when Thomas Brookes was landlord, the house was allowed to run down due to Brookes' dispute with his landlord. Brookes bought up the nearby Black Boy, and transferred most of his custom to that house. As a consequence the Woolpack closed down, and, its name being in abeyance, Brookes took it for his new house. Up the hill slightly was the Anchor, of 1767, used as the starting point of carriers to transport goods by wagon to and from Walsall. This old pub had been converted into a private house by May 1791, when it was put up for sale. Up between Phillips Street and Bell Street was the Boot, an early eighteenth-century public house. It was situated to one side of Rann's Yard, later the site of the Market Hall which opened in 1835. By 1786 the Boot had been renamed the Shovel.

On the other side of Phillips Street lay the Board Vaults. Up until the First World War it had an early morning market license, and opened at 6.00 a.m. Being near the Fish Market it

Above left: *A bill from the Dog Inn, 4 July 1792.*

Above right: *The Old Pump Tavern in the Bull Ring.*

Left: *A trade card of the Nelson, formerly the Dog, in the Bull Ring.*

was affectionately known as the 'Cod's Head'. During the 1880s it was known as Fox's, taking its name from a popular licensee. The house was taken over by Atkinson's Brewery at the end of the century. Just before the outbreak of the First World War its licensee was Anthony Diamond, who on 2 April 1886 became Amateur Heavyweight Champion of England. He successfully defended this title three times too. Needless to say there was never any trouble at Anthony Diamond's house. Diamond later went on to run the Great Western, next to Acock's Green Station. The license of the vaults was surrendered to the Justices in 1934, but the house was permitted to continue with a six-day license up to the redevelopment of the area for the 1960s Bull Ring Centre.

The last of Spiceal Street's taverns was the coaching inn, the Spread Eagle. The earliest record of this old timber-framed house was a deed of 1578, though the house was believed to have been much older. Francis Mole was landlord from 1767 to 1780. During his time the inn became an important coaching and carriers' house. A detailed description of the inn was given in its sales particulars in 1833:

> All that capital Freehold Inn, Liquor Shop, and well-frequented Market house
> With very extensive Stabling, large Granary, Warehouse, Yard, Gateway and
> Offices complete called the Spread Eagle Inn, in the Market Place, Birmingham,
> now in the possession of Mr. GRAY, who holds the same under a Lease granted
> many years ago to Messers. Hicken and Dunsford, which will expire Lady-day
> 1837, at the very low Rent of £120 per annum. This Lot embraces a large Frontage
> and contains between 700 and 800 square yards of Freehold Land.

Harry Bliss bought the pub and remained as licensee until post-1842. Later successor, William Cooper, opened a concert hall at the Spread Eagle in 1854. John Hannah, who was licensee during the 1880s, brought in architect William Robinson to draw up plans for improvements and additions to this old house, which he did on 30 April 1889. George Mallin was licensee during and after the First World War. The Spread Eagle finally closed in 1929, and Woolworth's shop was built on the site. This in turn was demolished for the building of the 1960s Bull Ring Centre.

At 8½ Bull Ring was the Wheatsheaf. It was approached down a wide entry opposite the church. It was a Georgian house, as an advertisement of 8 March 1742 indicates. This inn was also an important staging post for coaches and carriers. Deliveries were made from here, according to Sketchley's Directory of Birmingham for 1767, to Chester, Liverpool and Wigan. In the early nineteenth century father and son, Joseph and John Hoe, ran this tavern for the best part of thirty years. With John's departure the Wheatsheaf was renamed the Pump, taking its name from a public water pump nearby. An old man interviewed in the late nineteenth century for the periodical *Birmingham Faces and Places*, recollected that this old house had solid oak floors and furniture of a bygone era. That was to prove its problem. It had not kept up with the times; it could not compete, and so suffered financially. By the turn of the twentieth century it had became a common lodging house.

Built on an old burgage plot, the four-storey Comet, nearby, was a Georgian public house just opposite Nelson's statue in the Bull Ring. Its address was officially 5 High Street. Though narrow-fronted, it extended backwards to a depth of four rooms. For many years the Comet was only a beerhouse, and so was not recorded by name in the trade directories of the day. It was only with its purchase by Aston brewers, Holts, and becoming a tied house, did it gain a full license. The Comet surrendered its license to the Justices in 1928.

The Board, Spiceal Street, 1924.

The Comet, 5 High Street, 1924.

The old Royal George, c. 1958.

The Cock Inn was one of the original coaching inns of Birmingham, dating from the mid-sixteenth century. It was situated in Cock or Well Street, which is shown on William Westley's Plan of Birmingham for 1731, as being part of upper Digbeth High Street, abutting Park Street. As such it would appear to have been the fore-runner of the Royal George, at the junction of High Street and Park Street. According to the Hearth Tax returns of 1663, John Wall was landlord of the Cock, and in 1665, according to the Poor Law returns, it was owned by William Weeley, a Governor of King Edward School. The Town Book makes frequent reference to the house in the late seventeenth century.

All references to the Cock Inn cease by 1714, seeming to confirm the change in name to the Royal George, and a total rebuild of the property. William Dunn was recorded as innkeeper in Sketchley's Directory of 1767, the oldest surviving directory of Birmingham. Upon his death, his widow Sarah took over, and after her their daughters, 'The Misses Dunn'. The landlord of the George in 1779 was William Turner, who was forced to sell after he became bankrupt. Thomas Packwood was licensee in 1816, and post-1827 it was William Welch. William Huntriss followed in 1833, by which time the George was described as a 'commercial hotel'. Richard Bates followed him as licensee and Miss Hannah Maria Taylor took over from Bates. She is listed as licensee from 1851 to 1860. The George was then acquired by George Biber, who the following year renamed it the London Museum Tavern. Biber built a music hall onto the Park

The Royal George, 1967.

Street frontage, which opened on 24 December 1863 as the London Museum Concert Hall. In 1877 Donald MacInnes purchased the London Museum & Music Hall and ran it until 1887. Alex McGregor ran it for two years, or it may be that MacInnes put him in as manager, for in 1890 it is his name that appears in the trade directory when he renamed the inn the Canterbury Tavern. From 1894 to 1896 it was the Pavilion Tavern under Alfred Hardy and later Robert Hall.

In 1896 the pub was bought by brewers Henry Mitchell & Co. William Coutts purchased the music hall, which re-opened as Coutt's Theatre. With Richard Smith looking after the public house, Mitchell's undertook modernisation to the old inn, which reverted to its earlier name of the Royal George. Local pub architects, James & Lister Lea, were called in and prepared plans on 8 June 1896. The old building was refaced in brick and considerably altered. It was three storeys in height and very tall windows on the ground floor were opened up, flooding the inside with light. The main entrance was moved to the corner, but with two further entrances upon each street frontage. In 1900, following licensing difficulties, Couts Theatre was closed down. In 1912 the old music hall was converted into a cinema and renamed the Bull Ring Cinema. It closed in the 1930s, not being converted to 'Talkies'.

The Royal George, by then an M&B house, was closed on 3 January 1962, and was demolished when the Bull Ring Centre was constructed. The old music hall-cum-cinema was retained, and still exists, being used as the site office for the rebuilding of the Bull Ring in 2001-2. It is

St Martin's Tavern, c. *1970*.

probably the oldest purpose-built music hall building anywhere in this country. A new Royal George was built for M&B on the site of the former inn, set back a little from the road, and opened on 8 July 1964. Above its main entrance was a metal relief of an eighteenth-century ship of the line. This has since been removed following the closure of the pub in July 2005. At present the building remains boarded-up.

Skirting the southern end of the parish church is the crescent-shaped St Martin's Lane. At No. 4, on the corner with Moat Lane, was the Three Horse Shoes. It took its name from the Ferrer family, who had connections with the deBermingham family, thus establishing this house as a late medieval or early Tudor inn. It is listed in the oldest surviving trade directory for Birmingham for 1767. Thomas Chambers is given as licensee. He was followed by the Widow Chamberlain in 1777. William Jordan had succeeded as licensee by 1804. George Bearsley took over the house in 1827 and was here until 1855 when Joseph Marston took over. The old house was renovated in the Victorian era and received a new brick front. In 1928 the city council compulsorily purchased the site and the Horse Shoes was demolished for the construction of additional market warehouses.

The Swan with Two Necks, 8 St Martin's Lane, faced onto the parish church. Apparently dating from 1822, the house is depicted on a painted tile formerly in the Woodman in Easy Row. The view is dated 1840. The following year this corner of St Martin's Lane, bordering onto Edgbaston Street, was cleared in an early Improvement Scheme.

Perhaps the most interesting public house in this road was the Black Boy at 2 St Martin's Lane. The pub name refers to the dark-complexioned King Charles II. The inn was an impressive three-storey house, of seventeenth-century origins. The front entrance overlooked St Martin's churchyard. It was a typical provincial Georgian house, with central ground-floor door and arch surround, flanked by two large multi-paned bow windows. Above the doorway was a large lantern. This scene was captured in a pen and wash drawing by local artist A. Tarlington in 1870, when John Gough was landlord. The name was transferred sometime earlier from a public house just around the corner in Edgbaston Street. In 1767 the licensee of the Black Boy in St Martin's Lane was William Johnson. By 1803 the obituary of its then licensee, Thomas Bromley, refers to it as 'St Martin's Tavern and the Black Boy'. In a niche above the door, where a clock was afterwards placed, stood a well-modelled figure of a chubby Negro boy, his ebony skin as brilliant as varnish could make it; his lips bright with vermilion; his teeth white as snow; and the string of large beads encircling his neck doubly gilt and burnished, as Eliezer Edwards described it in his *Old Taverns of Birmingham*. The first portion of the house name was generally omitted. The tavern was popularly known as the Black Boy. In 1817, Thomas Brookes, who was then landlord of the Woolpack in Spiceal Street, was in dispute with his landlord. Just at that time the Black Boy was offered for sale, and Brookes succeeded in buying it. His lease at the Woolpack was due to expire in a few months time. Brookes removed to the Black Boy, but still kept the Woolpack on, which he proceeded to run down. All his old customers moved with him to the Black Boy. Consequently, when the lease on the Woolpack fell due, no one could be found to take it on. The inn closed, and the premises were sold to a tea dealer. The sign of the Woolpack having been abandoned, Mr Brookes altered the name of his new house to the Black Boy & Woolpack. Gradually the old name was dropped, and after a few years the figure of the Negro boy was removed, and the tavern became generally known as the Woolpack in St Martin's Lane. Brookes died in 1828 and was succeeded by a Mr Boddington, a former draper. In 1838 however, Brookes' son William took over. His widow continued the business after 1843, marrying wholesale butcher, John Gough, in 1848. Together they ran the house until his death in 1877. The Town Council negotiated the purchase of the house from his successor, auctioneer

49ers, formerly the Wandering Minstrel, c. 1984.

The Bull Ring Tavern, formerly an Ansell's house, 1974.

John Gilbert, buying it from him for £7,400. The old inn was demolished for the building of Smithfield Wholesale Vegetable Market. Upon completion of the scheme, a new hotel was built, whose frontage extended nearly the full length of St Martin's Lane. It was called St Martin's Hotel, harking back to the name of the original inn on the site. In the 1960s this hotel was demolished for the Bull Ring Shopping Centre.

The construction of the Bull Ring Centre in the early 1960s saw the clearing away of a number of old and much-loved public houses. Three new houses were built to replace them: the Matador, the Wandering Minstrel and the Bull Ring Tavern. The Matador was situated at the top of the spiral ramp, at an upper entrance into the shopping centre overlooking the parish church of St Martin. The house opened on 20 December 1963. Its license had been transferred from the closed down Crown at 50 Snow Hill. An M&B house, it became a Courage house in the great pub swap, and with the change, offered the attraction of Courage Directors. In the somewhat seedy Bull Ring Centre of 1995, the Matador was renamed the Blarney Stone. The second of the three, the Wandering Minstrel, was built at the bottom of an escalator entrance to the shopping centre. It too was an M&B house. As the 1990s drew on, it became 49ers, though the change of name hardly set the drinking world alight. Like the Matador, it was put out of its misery in the year 2000, with the building of the present Bull Ring Centre. The Bull Ring Tavern, the third of the new houses, was built on the corner of Moat Lane, St Martin's Lane and Digbeth High Street. It was built to replace the former St Martin's Hotel. Originally an Ansells house, it became a Courage house following the swap. Unlike the other two pubs it has a more traditional pub atmosphere, and is still very much a popular markets' pub.

An aerial view of the area of Birmingham city centre that lies within the Inner Ring Road.

TWO

INNER RING ROAD PUBS

The High Street and its Environs

Just above the Bull Ring, on the corner of High Street and New Street was Stevens' Bar. Its address was 80 High Street/140 New Street. Opened in 1916, under licensee Richard Marsh Williams, this pub was situated next door to the Swan Hotel. Inside it was impressively Edwardian, with stained glass, brass and mahogany. The 'atmosphere was heavily impregnated with mixed drinks, pipes, cigars, cigarettes and food that had been consumed by travellers for generations and seeped into the very fabric of the walls, ceilings, furniture and floors', a former local reminisced. 'It was unique. Tinned or bottled it would have been an export winner.' During the 1930s the Franco-British Electric Sign Co. erected a massive three-storey-high illuminated sign on the New Street frontage for owners M&B. At night time signs like these came into their own, epitomising the vibrancy of that inter-war era.

The top two storeys of the bar were badly damaged during the Blitz in 1941. They were demolished and house was capped off at first-floor level. The Swan next door was destroyed during the raid, save for its side entrance corridor, which, undamaged, was later incorporated into Stevens' Bar. In the post-war era, the Bar was a sad-looking little pub, partially boarded up on its New Street side for years. The small painted leaded lights, with their abstract flower designs, survived, still offering a hint of what Stevens' Bar once had been. It closed on the night of 25 March 1958, and was demolished soon after for the construction of the Inner Ring Road.

Crossing over the road to the other side of the High Street was the Lion & Lamb. It was situated down a yard between 19 and 20 High Street. Its first verifiable licensee according to the trade directory of 1767 was Thomas Harris. There is an obituary for William Morris on 4 April 1825. He is listed as 'of the Lion & Lamb'. His widow Lucy ran the pub until post-1837. The house came up for sale on 6 October 1852. Auctioneers Cheshire & Gibson described it as:

> The very spacious RETAIL SHOP and PREMISES, No. 16, in the High Street in the occupation of Mr Thomas Burbidge, seedsman and corn factor, and the well-accustomed Old-licensed PUBLIC HOUSE known as the LION AND LAMB, tenanted by Mr Hewett, with spare land at the rear. This lot has a frontage to High Street of 29 feet.

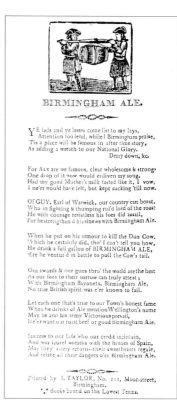

Above left: *John Freeth, poet and publican.*

Above right: *Freeth's Birmingham Ale.*

Mrs Hewett remained as licensee until 1864. The Rating Map of 1871 indicates that it was by then closed, and the license surrendered. It is described as 'not fit for use'. George Rickersby brought it back to use, and under licensee Albert Smith it underwent further updating, to the design of architect Thomas Plevins, in 1887. The Lion & Lamb was destroyed during the same enemy raid that damaged Stevens' Bar, in 1941.

Up on the corner where Waterstones bookshop now stands, was the Garland House at 26 High Street. The Garland House was the one-time home of Birmingham's first historian, William Hutton. He recorded that in 1772 he: 'purchased the Garland House … of wood and plaster … erected in 1567 … which I was obliged to take down.'

Hutton's date of 1567 would suggest a rebuild of an original medieval house, for in 1553 the Survey of Birmingham records that the site was the home of Thomas Smyth. The house later came into the possession of Samuel Porter and, as is witnessed in the Hearth Tax returns of 1663, the Garland House was renamed Porter's Coffee House. Under part of the building was a room measuring 45ft x 15ft, used as additional prison space to the Town Prison, then in the Toll Booth which stood immediately opposite. There is a suggestion that there was an earlier public house on the site, the Wyldicatte, in 1523. The Wild Cat, as we would now interpret the name, is referred to in Local Notes & Queries (*Birmingham Weekly Post*, 24 March 1949), unfortunately no source for the reference is given.

Stevens' Bar, on the corner of High Street and New Street, c. 1936.

Freehold and Leasehold Estates.

To be Sold by AUCTION,

By THOMAS WARREN,

On TUESDAY, the 14th of JULY 1789, precisely at Four o'Clock in the Afternoon.

At Mrs. *Lloyd's*, the *Hen and Chickens* Inn, *High-street*, Birmingham:

SUBJECT TO CONDITIONS THEN TO BE PRODUCED:

Lot I. THREE Leasehold TENEMENTS, or DWELLING HOUSES, with Shopping and other Outbuildings, two of which are fronting to the upper Side of St. Bartholomew's Chapel, near the End of Chapel-street, Birmingham, and one other in the Yard behind the said Front House, now or late in the respective Occupations of Thomas Brittain, Edward Hughes, and Joseph Hinsley, at several yearly Rents, amounting together to 21l. 16s. These Premises are held under a Lease, in which 36 Years will be unexpired at Michaelmas next, subject to an annual Ground Rent of 2l.

Lot II. Two LEASEHOLD TENEMENTS, or DWELLING HOUSES, situate in, and fronting to the lower End of Mole-street, Birmingham, aforesaid; and one other small Tenement in a Yard behind the said front Houses, now or late in the respective Occupations of Thomas Horton, Thomas Brown, Thomas Francis, Thomas Wren, at several yearly Rents amounting together to 18l. 18s. These Premises are held under a Lease, in which 57 Years were unexpired at Lady-day last, subject to an annual Ground Rent of 3l. 6s. 8d.

Lot III. Four FREEHOLD TENEMENTS, or DWELLING HOUSES, situate in Walmer Lane, Birmingham, aforesaid; now or late in the Occupations of Joseph Hunt, Mary Parkes, Thomas Pickens, and George Blunt, at the several yearly Rents, amounting together to 19l. 5s. together with a large Piece of vacant Land, part of the said Premises, on which great improvement might be made. These Premises are held under an annual Ground Rent of 2l. 10d.

Lot IV. Sundry GROUND RENTS, issuing out of certain new-erected Buildings, situate in Walmer Lane, and Lancaster Street, Birmingham, aforesaid; which produce a clear annual Income of 7l. 0s. 7¾d. for ever.

Lot V. Sundry other GROUND RENTS, issuing out of certain Premises situate in Park-street, Birmingham, aforesaid; which produces 1l. 10s. per annum.

Lot VI. A small LEASEHOLD TENEMENT, situate in the Balloon Yard, in Temple-street, Birmingham, aforesaid; now in the Occupation of William Goodby, at the yearly Rent of 5l. subject to an annual Ground Rent of 2s.

Lot VII. Two substantial modern-built DWELLING HOUSES, situate on, and fronting to Snowhill, Birmingham, aforesaid; one of which is commonly known by the Sign of the Indian Queen, in the Occupation of Mr. William Cox, under a Lease in which four Years and a half will be unexpired at Michaelmas next, at 18l. per Year, and the other in the Tenure of Mr. James Mears, as Tenant at will, at 13l. 13s. per Year; together with a large Stable, an extensive Range of Shopping, and other convenient Out-buildings. The whole of these Premises, which contain about 11 Yards in front, and upwards of 50 Yards in depth, are held under a Lease, in which 57 Years and 11 Months were unexpired the 24th Day of June last, subject to a Ground Rent of 3l. 6s. and are capable of great improvement.

Lot VIII. A LEASE in which ten Years will be unexpired at Michaelmas next, of a Dwelling House and Premises, being No 25, in Philip Street, Birmingham; nearly opposite the Bell, subject to the yearly Rent of seven Pounds, and now in the Occupation of Mr. William Walker, as Tenant at will, at 9l. 9s. per Year.

Lot IX. A LEASE in which fifteen Years and a half will be unexpired at Michaelmas next, of that commodious well accustomed Public House, commonly known by the Sign of the SWAN, in Smallbrook Street, Birmingham—Together with another Tenement adjoining, in which 16 Years will be unexpired at Michaelmas next, subject to the small annual Rent of 19l. 1s.—The whole of these Premises are now in the Occupation of Mr. William Ward, or his under Tenants, at 21l. per Year.

☞ Further Particulars may be known by applying to the Auctioneer, in Dale End, Birmingham.

BIRMINGHAM; PRINTED BY BROWN AND BENTLEY, NEW-STREET.

Left: An auction at the Hen & Chickens in the High Street, 1789. Note Lot VII, the Indian Queen.

Below: The Hen & Chickens, New Street, 1800.

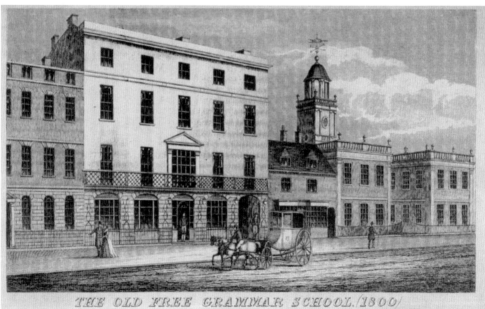

THE OLD FREE GRAMMAR SCHOOL /1800/
& LLOYD's New HOTEL, & Hen & Chickens Inn, BIRMINGHAM.

Situated a few doors along the High Street from the Garland House was the Star. It was in existence by 1702. Nearby was the Angel, one of the oldest inns in Birmingham. At one time the affluent Colmore family owned it. William Colmore is recorded as owner of the 'Aungell' in 1566. The Pemberton family acquired the inn in the late seventeenth century. John Pemberton was licensee in 1663, according to the Hearth Tax returns. The family leased the Angel, first of all to Thomas Rogers in 1676, and later to John Rhoades in 1693. Then owner, Roger Pemberton, was also a goldsmith, and kept 'Running Cash', a euphemism for acting as a banker. In 1723 this old timber-framed house was faced in brick and renamed the Hen & Chickens, the name under which it was sold to Robert Corbett in 1724 for £300. To many it remained the old Angel, even some twenty years after. In 1742 the departure place for the London Coach to the Rose Inn at Holborn Bridge is given as 'The Angel and Hen and Chickens, in the High Town'.

By 1784 Richard Lloyd was landlord. Upon his death his widow carried on the business until the termination of her husband's lease in 1798. For whatever reason she did not renew the lease, but instead removed to a new house in New Street and took the Hen & Chickens name with her.

The new hotel was designed by John Wyatt and built that same year. It was three storeys in height, with five bays and a balconied front, all clad in stone. In 1804 William Waddell purchased the inn. He had the front remodelled and a portico added. Upon Waddell's death in 1836 the hotel was sold for £14,500. A Mr Devis took out a lease on it for £600 a year. He in his turn sub-let it to a Mrs Room at £700 a year. In 1849 Frank Smith took up the lease. Under him it became a nationally known coaching inn where Charles Dickens, William Macready the actor-manager, novelist Wilkie Collins, actress Mrs Siddons, musician Paganini, Louis Napoleon (afterwards Napoleon III) and the great Irish politician, Daniel O'Connell, all stayed, and where thirty stagecoaches called daily. The last landlord was Mr Oldfield, who took possession in 1867, and conducted the business until the end of its lease in 1878. That year the premises in New Street were acquired by the Birmingham Aquarium Co. Ltd, who demolished the building and proposed to erect a handsome concert room, aquarium and restaurant. Their plans came to nothing, and the site was boarded up. The site was later acquired by the Birmingham Coffee House Co. Ltd in January 1896. A new Hen & Chickens Hotel was built in the Gothic style in red terracotta, to a design by the Birmingham architect J.A. Chatwin. The new hotel was opened in 1898. It was modernised and extended in the late 1930s. A change in name to the Arden Hotel came about because the teetotal company felt that the old name sounded more like a licensed house. The Arden was further modernised during the 1950s, but its lack of an alcohol license proved its downfall. Trade dropped off and the hotel was forced to close. The Arden was demolished in 1972.

At 22 High Street in 1845 was a licensed premise, the Peeping Tom. The trade directory of that year lists William Preston as its landlord. At 39-40 was the Bodega, a popular restaurant with a public bar. It was owned by the Bodega Co. Ltd. In July 1914 they sold the business as a going concern. The sales catalogue details the premises:

No. 39 High Street, with the Extensive Bar, Smoke Room and Premises in the rear thereof, and the floors over Nos. 39 and 40, High Street, let to the Bodega Company Ltd., ...upon Repairing Lease, for a term of twenty-one years from the 25th day of March 1906, at an annual rent of £575 ...The Premises comprise large Wine Cellar with Back Entrance, Lavatory, and two w.c.'s, and a second Cellar in the Basement.

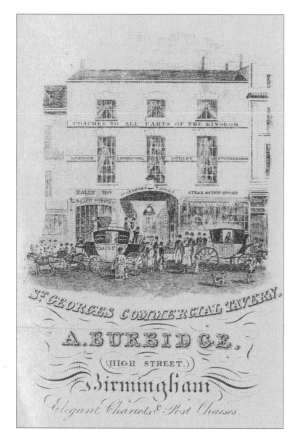

Above left: *St George's Tavern in the High Street.*

Above right: *Alfred Aston, licensee of the Red Lion, 1902.*

The license of the Bodega was surrendered to the Licensing Justices in 1925, but its termination was held in abeyance until July 1959, when the Bodega closed, and the license was transferred to the Birmingham Co-operative Society Ltd Wines and Spirits Department.

Two doors further on, though several centuries earlier, was the Reindeer, at what was to become 41 High Street. A mid to late seventeenth-century inn, its licensee in 1663 was John Moorland. In 1691 it became a coaching inn. There is an advertisement to this effect in the *London Gazette* for 7-11 May:

> There is a stage-coach goes from the Rain-Deer Inn, in Birmingham, every Monday Morning, 6 o'clock, going through Warwick and Banbury, and comes to the Bell Inn, in West-Smithfield, every Wednesday, and so returns every Thursday, to the Rain-Deer Inn, in Birmingham, every Saturday at 18s. each Passenger. Performed by Nich. Rothwell, of Warwick.

Two years later, in 1693, the building was refaced in brick by builder Richard Pinley. In the early eighteenth century the house was renamed the Castle Inn. Dr Samuel Johnson stayed here in the autumn of 1734. In the stable belonging to the inn was held the first theatrical performance in the town under a permanent cover, before a dedicated theatre was erected in Moor Street. John Camden was landlord here between 1767 and 1770. On 22 May 1769 the first meeting of the Commissioners of the Birmingham Lamp Act took place at the Castle Inn, where apparently they continued to meet for some time thereafter. Samuel Lloyd succeeded Camden. A Mr Piper ran this coaching inn after Lloyd. His widow continued until her retirement in 1785. John Ibberson, whose father ran the George & Blue Boar in Holborn, London, bought the house. During his time the Castle acted as the meeting place of the magistrates during the Scarcity Riots of 1800. Ibberson was succeeded by another Londoner, William Waddell, who later took over the rival coaching inn, the Hen & Chickens in New Street. When put up for sale in 1812, an advertisement in the *Birmingham Gazette* (12 October) revealed that the Castle had four dining rooms and twenty-three bedrooms. William Chapman took over the license, he was followed by John and Thomas Law, and finally, William Felton. The Castle was closed in 1854. Edward Gem, an export merchant, purchased one part, Joseph Barrow the other. Barrow took over the Castle's license, put in new windows, and opened a wine and spirits merchants called the Castle Vaults. This closed down in May 1922.

The long narrow alleyway to the side of the Vaults was known as Castle Street. In its time it supported three public houses. The earliest was the Fox, whose licensee in 1767 was John Key. At 15 Castle Street was the Golden Elephant. In 1834 William Lowe was listed as its landlord. This house appears to have closed in 1879. At the lower end of Castle Street, on the corner with Moor Street, was the Iron House, established by 1880.

Back to the High Street, at 43 was Knapp's Hotel, opened in 1859 by Stephen Knapp. After his departure the hotel retained its original name, owing to the popularity of its former owner. The house finally closed in 1900. Next door, at 44 High Street, was the St George's Tavern, a large three-storey coaching inn, with central gateway leading into a yard. It dated from *c*.1800. The licensee of the tavern throughout most of the first twenty years of the nineteenth century was George Gervus Wood, previously landlord of licensed premises in Moor Street from 1767 up to 1797. George G. Wood died on 4 November 1820. The death of his successor, William Burbidge, is recorded in the *Gazette* for 25 October 1827. His widow Ann continued to look after the tavern after his death. In 1855 John Chadwick was licensee. Thomas Blakoe followed Chadwick as landlord, and he in turn was followed by Job Winchurch in 1862. Charles Henry Hobday was landlord 1864-8, and Samuel Smith, 1868-70. During his time the name changed to the St George's Vaults. About this time the building was divided up, only part of it remained as a public house. Mrs Ellen Beck became landlady in 1871, and Thomas Parton became landlord in 1875. Edward Musto was the last licensee. The house closed in 1880. A new public house, the Holborn, on the corner of Corn Exchange Passage, opened some four and a half years later, in 1885. The Holborn's first licensee was Samuel P. Robotham. He was followed by Fred Wright in 1888, who remained as landlord until 1903. Frank Ruck then took up the license of what had become an Ansells tied house. The Holborn closed in 1929. Situated just the other side of the Passage was the Corn Exchange Vaults, at 46 High Street. It opened in 1854, and closed when its lease expired on 30 December 1933.

Also closed on that same day was the Albion Commercial Hotel, on the corner of Carr's Lane. It opened in 1858 under licensee Charles Bullivant. He was landlord here for over thirty years, and by 1864 the house was known as Bullivant's Hotel, the name that it was to retain thereafter until its closure. On the corner of High Street and Carr's Lane was the eighteenth-century Crown, at 5 Carr's Lane. William Ball was licensee from 1787 to 1797. In the 1791 directory he is described as a 'victualler and cheese & salt factor'. He died in 1809. James Hughes was later

The Red Lion, on the corner of High Street and New Meeting Street, 1958.

landlord, from 1828 to 1842. At 14 Carr's Lane was the Turk's Head. This house dated from *c.* 1820, when Charles Harrold was recorded as its licensee. His widow Elizabeth took over following his death in 1838, and ran the house for the next decade. It was closed for the construction of a railway tunnel to what was to become Snow Hill Station. Long gone by that time, presumably, was the third public house here, the Rose, at 21 Carr's Lane. It was open in the 1780s. Jeremiah Stevens was licensee from 1780 to post-1787.

In this stretch of the High Street between New Street and Carr's Lane was situated the Mitre. It was in existence in the mid-eighteenth century when this part of the High Street was known as the Beast, or Rother Market. *Aris's Gazette* for 29 August 1743 records the sale of its lease:

> To be Lett, in Birmingham, the Mitre Inn, in the Beast Market, completely repaired, with good Stabling, and large Cellars, and a Brewhouse, and a Chamber, over it in the Yard; a good Well, and other Conveniences, fit for an Inn. To be enter'd upon immediately. Enquire of Mr Holloway; or of Mr Simcox, Attorney-at-law, in Birmingham.

Other un-numbered pubs in the High Street include the Half Moon and Swan, a carriers pub, listed in the trade directory of 1767, under John Nicholls, the Malt Shovel of 1818, with licensee George Walton, and The Shades of 1865, whose licensee was Charles Hobday.

The Red Lion was on the corner of High Street and New Meeting Street, Dale End. It was an old house rebuilt in Victorian times. To the faithful it was known as 'Clements', having been in the possession of that family for half a century. The Red Lion began life in 1780, Thomas Smith being listed in the trade directory of that year as its licensee. Its original address was given as 3 New Meeting Street. Smith died in January 1786. The following year John Constable took up the license. He was there until 1791. William Pimlott took over the Red Lion from him. By the time of the 1799 directory Pimlott had been replaced by William Uphill. He died in October 1812. His widow Mary ran the business up to 1828, thereafter their son, Edward took over. In the mid-Victorian period the house is sometimes listed as the Red Lion (Vaults) at 58 High Street. In July 1899, when the house was offered for sale, it was described as being:

> Handsome and of modern design, having been entirely re-built some few years since and consists of Spacious wine and spirit vaults, with Street Frontage of 73 feet, and having a well-proportioned dining or sitting room over, with Private Office, Five Bed Chambers, Kitchens, Pantries and usual Domestic Accommodation, and cool Ale and Spirit Cellars in the Basement.

The house was snapped up by Ansells to add to their stable of tied houses. The Red Lion was a cosy sort of pub, a local in the city centre, with bar and smoke-room, and an eclectic clientele. In March 1977 a planning application was submitted to demolish it and build a two-storey shopping block on the site. Despite a vigorous protest, and an attempt to get it listed, this popular town pub was demolished.

Down the narrow alleyway that is New Meeting Street were two public houses, the Plume of Feathers and the Coach & Horses. The Feathers appears to have been a beerhouse, and as such was not listed in the trade directories. It is only with the obituary of its owner, Joseph Young, landlord from 1798 to 1803, that we learn of its existence. Further down was the Coach & Horses at 6 New Meeting Street. It was a narrow-fronted Georgian three-storey house, with plain windows either side of a central door. Charles Yarwood was licensee from 1823. In 1852, the fantastically named Neptune Henry Stagg was its landlord. The Coach & Horses was offered for sale by auction on 8 December 1885, where it is described as being:

... in a very central position near the principal thoroughfares of the town of Birmingham, with Yard and Outbuildings, let to Mr George Wilde, on a repairing lease for the remainder of a term of Fourteen years from Michaelmas 1874 at a yearly rent of £57 10s. This is an important and valuable Public-house, and offers an excellent and improving Freehold Investment, and particularly so for the surplus capital of Brewers.

Brewers, Showell & Son, bought the Coach & Horses. In 1894 they commissioned C.J. Holloway to update their acquisition. He made minor alterations to the street frontage, and added a closet toilet for the comfort of its patrons. In 1917 the Coach & Horses was closed following the recommendation of the Licensing Justices.

Returning to the High Street, just a short way further on, is Albert Street. A short way down, on the corner with Moor Street, was the Old Bell. It began life in 1853. Edward Grimley was its first landlord. He held the license until his death in 1863. His widow took over for a year, before selling to William Marshall. The Old Bell closed in 1867. Back up to the High Street, and across the road, was the Fox & Dogs, at 59 High Street. It was situated next door to the old Lamb House. From 1767 to 1777, this house was run by the appropriately named Ann Fox. Further down the road, heading back towards the Bull Ring, was the Wine & Spirit Vaults of Mrs Peters at 101 High Street, and two doors down from there was John Bridcut's Wine & Spirits Vaults also dating from 1865. At 105 High Street was the Seven Stars, dating from the mid-eighteenth century. The landlord of the house, in 1766, and for the next decade, was Thomas Hubbard. He died in November 1777. The 'Widow Hubbard' as she is referred to in the directory, took over and remained as mistress of the house until her death in June 1797. The Boot was at 108 High Street, with Jane Brown as licensee from 1767 to 1774. Lastly, at 110 High Street, at the same time, 1767 to 1770, under Joseph Barnsley, was the Crispin, named after the patron saint of cobblers and shoemakers.

Dale End

Today there are just two public houses in Dale End, The Hole in the Wall and Scruffy Murphy's. The earliest known of the Dale End pubs was the Peacock in Welch End, listed in the Birmingham Survey of 1553. The Welch End, at the junction of High Street, and Bull Street, was so-called because it was here that the Welsh cattle and sheep drovers sold their beasts. Other houses without precise locations include the Old Bird in Hand, of 1767, with John Groutage as licensee. In January 1794, then landlord Richard Spreadborough offered the attraction of an armadillo on display! Another licensee, Thomas Blakemore, reputedly lived to be 105 years old. Then there was the Brown Lion, a licensed victullers, who's licensee, Abraham Horton, died on 2 June 1802; the Star & Bull's Head, which evolved into the Bull's Head, there from 1800 to 1818; the Blue Bell, with Ann Bott as licensee, 1817-20; and the Golden Lion, with William Cheshire as landlord from 1840 to his death in June 1847.

At 19 Dale End, on the eastern side of the road, was the Coach & Horses, listed in the trade directories from 1818 to 1869. At 38 Dale End was the Green Lamp, opened in 1875 with David Gilbert as licensee. There was the Boar, an 1850s public house, which evolved into the Board by the 1880s. Its original address was 95 Dale End. The house closed in 1906.

The Engine Inn, at 49 Dale End, was a low two-and-a-half-storey house, its building materials reputedly came from the demolished Priory, around the corner in Bull Street. If true, this would suggest a construction date of around 1540. As to its name, an old print shows the inn sign as what appears to be a pump, topped by a wheel. Underneath the picture is inscribed:

> I hope my engine will never fail,
> To draw my friends good beer and ale.

In the print John Richards is shown as its licensee, thus dating the picture to 1861-1866. William Shaw was the first positively identified landlord of the Engine Inn, in 1785. In the *Birmingham Gazette* of 18 July, he advertises that the house is:

> newly fitted up at large expense … that in order to render it worthy of patronage, the whole business will be conducted on the genteelest and most liberal plan – Good beds and stabling, the most genuine liquors and the choicest accommodation of all kinds will be constantly provided.

The Old Engine, as it had become, situated near the corner with Masshouse Lane, was subject to alterations and updating by architect William Wykes, during 1881, for licensee Thomas Stevens. During his stewardship the house became a noted Army recruiting house. This old house was closed in 1917 and the site was redeveloped. At 50 Dale End was the Coffee Pot, its landlord from 1767 to 1777 was Christopher Earl.

There was a stone cross in Dale End known as the 'stub Cross', so-called because only its stub remained by 1730. Two pubs took their name from this cross, the Red Stone Cross and the Old Stone Cross. The Red Stone Cross was a beerhouse, dating from the eighteenth century. One hundred years later in May 1886, William Ward undertook improvements to this house. The Old Stone Cross, originally the Stone Cross, is verifiable from 1795 at least, where William Smith is listed as a licensed victualler. He was licensee up to October 1800. Longstanding landlord, Robert Owen, took over in 1835. Under him the Old Stone Cross was home to the Churchwardens' Club, and was reputedly visited by Charles Dickens. Alterations were carried out to the Cross by William Wykes in 1887 and under brewers, Holt's, C.H. Collett carried out further work in June 1899. Then an Ansells tied house, it was eventually demolished in 1961 for the building of Priory Queensway as part of the Inner Ring Road.

Across the road from the Old Engine was the Wine & Spirit Vaults at 77 Dale End. It was situated on the corner of Newton Street. In existence by 1865, when Richard Dodds was licensee, about 1867 it changed its name to the Horse & Groom. Thomas Ireland had taken charge by then. The house surrendered its licence to the Justices in 1883 as part of the Improvement Scheme.

At 81 Dale End was the Golden Cross. It was a licensed victuallers and home-brew house, under Victorian licensee Bill Smith. The Golden Cross dated from 1767. Its first recorded landlord, and up to 1777, was George Morris. One-time landlord, William Owen, was a friend of the novelist Charles Dickens, who in 1852 visited Birmingham, disguised as a common working man, in order to study the habits and sayings of Birmingham people. During his stay he visited the Golden Cross. One night as he was leaving, disguised as he was, he called over his shoulder, 'Goodnight gaffer'. To his surprise Owen called back, 'Goodnight Charlie'. Dickens turned and returned to the bar, 'Do you know me?' he asked. Owens replied that he did, to which Dickens asked that he should tell no one. Owen agreed, and the two men became friends.

The Old Engine, Dale End, based on a sketch of 1865.

In the autumn of 1913 the Golden Cross featured in an advertisement in the *Birmingham Echo*:

Peter Troman. Golden Cross, Dale End. Member of the License Holders' Angling Society. FREE HOUSE. Bass Bitter from the wood, No.1; No.4 mild; and other noted ales. Bass and Guinness in bottle. The finest brands of Wines, Spirits and Cigars all mellow and matured. Newly renovated bars, snug and smoke room. Assembly room seat 3000 free to good society. Social Club, Monday. Dinners and Cold Snacks.

The Golden Cross was closed down five years later in 1918.

Demolition of the Old Engine, Dale End.

W. SMITH,

" GOLDEN CROSS, "

81, DALE END, BIRMINGHAM.

FOREIGN WINES AND SPIRITS,

OF THE BEST QUALITY.

Fine Home-brewed and Burton Bitter Ales ; London and Dublin Stout on draught and in bottles.

Above: *An advertisement for the Golden Cross, Dale End, 1866.*

Opposite: *The Old Stone Cross, Dale End, c. 1960.*

The Swan nearby, at 84 Dale End, also dated from 1767, William Kiss being its earliest known licensee. From 1775 until its closure in 1780, it was run by Thomas Blakemore.

The Leopard was at 87 Dale End. Despite a very narrow frontage onto the street, the Leopard stretched back to some depth with a series of rooms. It was the one-time sporting house of Morris Roberts. A permanent fixture in the pub was Peter Morris, one-time Lightweight Champion of England. He took part in some of the boxing matches that were held here on a regular basis. Roberts himself was a gifted amateur boxer himself. The Leopard was established as a public house by 1767, when William Farr was listed as its licensee. In 1899 Holt Brewery, who then owned the house, commissioned Birmingham architect C.H. Collett to update it, giving it a new frontage. In 1917 the Justices closed down a number of houses in the area, including the Leopard.

The Bell was situated on the corner of Stafford Street. There was a public house here by the mid-eighteenth century. James Jackson was licensee in 1767. William Crow and his wife, Ann, ran the house from 1825 until 1838. It was during the time of amateur boxer Morris Roberts that the house derived a degree of notoriety. Roberts was an admirer of William Murphy, an anti-Roman Catholic bigot. There was a riot, allegedly led by Roberts. Later when a Catholic entered the Bell to remonstrate with Morris, he drew a revolver and shot him dead. At his subsequent trial Robert's pleaded self-defence against the unarmed man – and got off! In the late Victorian period the house was rebuilt on a grand scale in red brick and terracotta. Four storeys in height, the new house was designed with two small towers either side of its corner entrance. In 1962 the license of the house was surrendered to the Justices, and the premises were

41

The Star Wine Vaults, The Exchange and the State Cabin, Dale End, 1898.

converted into shops and offices. The building was later demolished for the reconstruction of Dale End in the mid-1960s.

The Nottingham Arms, formerly the Nottingham Vaults, a licensed victuallers, was situated at 95 Dale End. The house originated in 1874, with William Slim as its first licensee. It closed in 1917. Saint Peter's Tavern at 100 Dale End, took its name from the nearby church, consecrated in 1827. The pub itself dated from 1839. Ambrose Winder was its first, and possibly only, licensee. At 105 Dale End was the Waggon & Horses. Its earliest recorded licensee was Abraham Dutton, who ran this public house from 1767 to 1780. During this period the house was used by carriers to take goods to London, and points along the way. Dutton retired to Five Ways, where he died on 15 September 1809. Richard Lawson succeeded him. He remained until his death in September 1805. Alterations were carried out under architect William Jenkins, who drew up plans in June 1881. The old house was given a new Victorian front with large etched windows. Long gone by Jenkins' conversion was the nearby Cross Guns, at the junction of Lower Priory. It had closed in the mid-1840s. The house is first recorded in the directory of 1783 under-maltster Samuel Smith. He remained here until 1823. The Cross Guns' last licensee was John Ryland.

In the grouping of buildings between 109 and 118 Dale End (Lower Priory to Bull Street), there were five licensed premises according to the Rating Maps of 1870. At 110 Dale End was the Red Cow, a three-storey Regency house. It is first recorded in the Birmingham directory of 1812. William Baylis was listed as licensee. George Jackson, its one-time licensee, died at the Red Cow on 22 March 1832. In 1861, under licensee John Haydon, the house was updated and renamed the State Cabin. In 1917 it and four other houses in Dale End were recommended for closure by the Licensing Justices as part of their 'fewer but better' scheme.

Three doors up from the Red Cow was the Royal Exchange at 113 Dale End. This was another licensed victuallers and dated from about 1822. The Royal Exchange fell victim to the whims of the Licensing Justices and was likewise closed in 1917.

Immediately next door at 114 Dale End was the Star Wine Vaults, another licensed victuallers. It appears as The Star in the trade directory of 1812, with Samuel Chandler as its landlord. The house was an unprepossessing three-storey building, erected about the same time as its next door neighbour. Despite its later change in name to the Star Wine Vaults, it continued to sell beer. In a late nineteenth-century photograph the house is shown advertising Burton-brewed Allsop's 60-shilling Ale, and Stout – presumably Guinness. By 1905 the Star, then an M&B house, was known as the Star Vaults. Unlike its near neighbours, the house was not closed down in 1917, but survived into the 1960s. The Star closed on 6 July 1966 for the redevelopment of Dale End. Its license was transferred to the Cabin in Priory Queensway.

The Liverpool Stores, two doors up from the Star Vaults, was apparently a beerhouse. Joseph Newport was licensee in 1861, remaining there until 1866 at least. The house is shown, and marked 'P.H.' on the Rating Map of 1870, but its name is not given. Like the un-named beerhouse next door, it was closed down in 1917.

The replacements for those pubs now gone, are the Hole in the Wall and Scruffy Murphy's. The Hole is an M&B house dating from the early 1970s. There are two bars – both blasted by loud music, and the place is usually packed by the younger element. Scruffy Murphy's, originally the Pen & Wig, took its name from the nearby Law Courts. It was built below the Priory Ringway, next to the National Car Park. A lunchtime pub, in the evening it can be quiet; rather like visiting the *Marie Celeste*.

Bull Street

The name of the street is taken from a public house, the Bull, which dated back to the sixteenth century. The Bull was situated at what is now the entrance to Temple Row. Henry Sedgwick was landlord of the house from 1535 until sometime after 1547. He sold the inn to John Vesey and retired to Sutton Coldfield. Vesey settled the Bull on near relative Symon Vesey, who, dying in 1614, left it to his son Edward. Sometime before 1630, Sir Thomas Holte of Aston Hall acquired it. The house was leased to Zachary Taylor, and then to his son, Richard. The Bull was damaged by fire during the Civil War. It was rebuilt in 1648, and in a renewal of the lease the original name of the house was revealed to be the Hart's Head. After the Restoration, Sir Robert Holte sold the Bull to Bishop Smallbrook. The Quaker developer, John Pemberton, purchased the inn from the Smallbrook family in 1698. The old house was pulled down when Temple Row was cut, to give access to the new St Philip's church, opened in 1715.

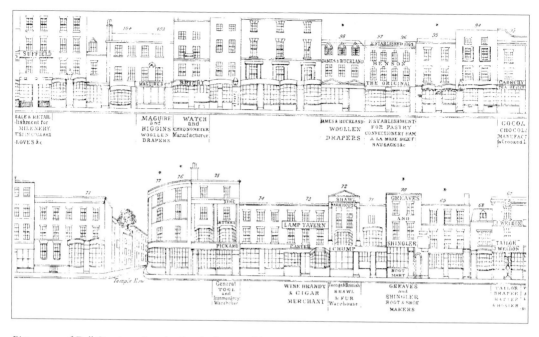

Picture map of Bull Street, c. 1825, showing the Lamp at No. 73.

Near the junction of Dale End and Lower Bull Street was the Blue Bell at 8 Bull Street. John Latham was licensee between 1767 and 1777. At 20 Bull Street was Skelton's Vaults, established by 1880 under licensee Alfred Goode. Its license was abandoned in 1883 for the cutting of Corporation Street. After the rebuilding, the street numbering was modified, and in the relocation of numbers, 20 Bull Street later became the Falstaff. The house dated from 1902, with Ambrose Sinclair as its first licensee. Originally a Holt's tied house, it was a licensed victuallers, which successfully extended its licensing hours under the Licensing Act of 1923. The Falstaff closed in 1961 when Lower Bull Street was being redeveloped.

The Saracen's Head was situated at 25 Bull Street, just below the present junction with Corporation Street. It was an old timber-framed coaching inn, later encased in brick. Its windows were low and irregular, suggesting its early seventeenth-century origins. In 1803 the Birmingham Directory records that the inn was the starting place for coaches to London, Bristol, Bath, Liverpool, Carlisle and Glasgow. By the 1830s with the arrival of the railways, the days of the coaching inns were numbered. The Saracen's Head was no exception. But if old houses were closing, then new ones were opening. The Globe, three doors down from the entrance to the Quaker Meeting House, at 39 Bull Street, opened in 1867. Samuel Welton Johnson was the licensee. In 1891 the Globe was bought by Thomas Whitehouse. His company, Whitehouse Brothers, then ran the house until its closure in 1914.

Just in the Minories was another old house, the Bull's Head, known for its tripe suppers, served in a large, low-ceilinged bare-boarded dining room. It survived well into the twentieth century. The Rose & Punchbowl, at 41 Bull Street, was a narrow-fronted house stretching back from the street for some distance to the Quaker burial ground behind. The Rose & Punchbowl appears to have originated in the eighteenth century. In 1800 the house was listed as the starting point for carriers to the north of England. Edward Collins was licensee then, and up to 1807.

44

John Jones was later listed as licensee, dying here in 1837. His wife Ann continued to run the house. James and Mary Hughes followed, taking the house into the twentieth century. The Rose & Punchbowl closed in 1904, was partially rebuilt and updated, and re-opened as the Scotch House under licensee Wilfred Wright. He remained here for thirteen years before being replaced by Frank Ruck. The house closed in 1934.

Three doors up was the Beehive, which started life in the eighteenth century as the Ship & Rainbow. Its first verifiable licensee was Matthias Webb, landlord from 1791 until his death in February 1797. During the occupancy of his successor, Thomas Emberton, the pub became a carriers' house for wagons travelling to the north. Emberton died in 1808. The Ship & Rainbow was renamed the Rainbow & Beehive, post-1835. John Barnett was responsible for the name change. He was landlord up to 1847. James Reynolds took over and the house was refurbished, re-opening as the Beehive. The pub operated on a six-day license – closed on Sunday. Taken over by Atkinson's Brewery, the old house was demolished and rebuilt to the design of James & Lister Lea. Their creation was a grand Classical four-storey house, completely different from their other turn of the century red brick and terracotta public houses. The Beehive closed in the 1950s for the renovation of this part of Bull Street.

At 51 Bull Street was the Coffee Tavern, perversely a beerhouse. It does not appear in the directories under its name, but came to light when, in January 1891, James Moffatt submitted plans for improvements. On or about this site was the Bell of 1767. An advertisement of that year reveals that carriers operated from here to the Black Country.

Across on the other side of the road at 67 Bull Street was the Lamp. It was a three-storey Georgian house three doors up from Temple Row, and dating from 1760. The first known licensee was Richard Jones. He appears as landlord from 1767 to 1777. His son, also called Richard Jones, took over and ran the house until 1807. When the Lamp came up for sale by auction on 27 January 1820 it was described as :

A most desirable and important house, the situation of which as a Tavern, Coach and Travellers' Inn, as well as a general Public House, in undeniably the best in the Town of Birmingham, and the sum required to take possession is comparatively small.

Francis Carver was licensee from 1829 to 1846. During his tenancy the Lamp is mentioned in the Grand Junction Railway Companion for 1838 as providing 'a substantial dinner set out for 1s. per head.' The Georgian building in which the Lamp was housed is shown in a street panorama of *c.* 1850.

Three generations of the Matthews family held the house from 1852 to 1884. Frederick Menzies bought the Lamp in 1885 for £5,500. During his tenancy, in 1887 architect William Wykes remodelled the front of the building, producing a rather splendid Victorian street frontage of stained and etched glass. The Lamp closed on 4 February 1958 and was converted into a shoe shop.

The Nelson at 77 Bull Street was situated on the corner of 4 Temple Row. It opened in 1905, the centenary of Nelson's victory at Trafalgar. Richard Hamley was its first licensee. He was followed by his son John, and he by Samuel Dodd in 1909. By the 1930s the house was known as Ye Olde Nelson. It and the other buildings along this stretch of the road were redeveloped in the late 1950s and early 1960s.

Across on the other corner of Bull Street and Temple Row was the Swan. Over the years it was also known as Peters', taking its name from the 1860s Mary Peters' Wine & Spirit Vaults. As the Swan it dated from *c.* 1770. John Southall was landlord here until his retirement in 1791.

The house became the Board in 1869 under licensee William Osborne. It was given a new front and updated to serve the modern requirements of a licensed victuallers. A popular lunchtime venue, its license was withdrawn in 1918. The licensee of the day was paid a generous £943 in compensation for lost earnings, in this prosperous part of the town. Also paid, but not so generously, in the previous year, was Frank Bridges, the licensee of the Fonda Bar, at 95 Bull Street. The house had been established some twenty years prior by the Beresford Brothers in 1897. The house was closed by the Justices in 1917. Bridges, who had only been licensee for a short time, received only £15. A few doors down at 88 Bull Street was the licensed victuallers, the London Restaurant. It surrendered its license in 1883.

At 92 Bull Street was the Chain. Advertised for sale in 1779, the Chain had 'stabling for upward of fifty horses and a convenient room for tradesmen'. Its purchaser was Charles Wells. There is an obituary for landlord Edward Banks in the *Gazette* of 4 May 1795. The last landlord appears to have been William Vickers, who died on 24 September 1801. This old public house was closed soon after, and became shops. By 1806 it had become 'Mr Newbold's Dancing Academy'.

The Turtle, a beerhouse, was at 98 Bull Street in 1864; Charles Benson was its licensee. On the corner with High Street was the Lamb, in the Lamb Yard. It was an old timber-framed house with an equally long history. From 1631 to 1645, its landlord was Robert Standford. Josiah Carpenter, a former baker, was licensee in 1660. He leased the premises from Sarah Caldecott, a widow, then living in Nuneaton. By 1690 the house was leased to Josiah's widow, Sarah, who by that date had remarried a man by the name of John Roades. In that year he erected additional stables and other outhouses. The Lamb ceased to trade as a public house by 1772, when a deed of that year shows that the building had been subdivided.

Of unknown location were three houses, the Bear, the Bear & Ragged Staff, and the George. The Bear was a carriers' inn, dating from 1767 to post-1800. It was particularly noted for its inn sign, depicting a great bear, painted on either side. One side was 'done by an eminent portrait painter of the name of Miller', Bisset's Magnificent Directory informs us, 'and the obverse by Moses Houghton, celebrated for his paintings of fish and dead game'. Of the Bear & Ragged Staff there is little information. It was a late eighteenth-century carriers inn. Lastly the George, an early eighteenth-century brick-built house, its earliest known licensee was a Mrs Dukes, whose death notice appears in the *Gazette* for 26 June 1797. Her husband, Richard, is listed as a licensed victualler here some twenty years prior. The last entry for this house is in 1821.

Snow Hill

Snow Hill is the north-westerly continuation of Bull Street. It was developed from c. 1730. There were a number of eighteenth-century public houses built here before street numbering had been introduced. There was the Blue Bell, flourishing in 1767 with Jonathan England as licensee; the White Lion, again 1767, with Edward Gibbons as licensee; the Nag's Head, another 1760s pub with William Bonnington; the Rising Sun, with Joseph Baker; three separate Lamp Taverns all in the 1765-1777 period; one for definite was at 10 Snow Hill, with William Osbourne as licensee from 1767 to 1777. A little later was the Horse & Groom of 1797. Then there was the Neptune, run by Edward Taylor from 1805-9. The Brown Lion was run by Joseph Brunner in 1818. Born in Germany, but later naturalised, Brunner was better known as a musical box and wooden clock maker. The last of the un-numbered houses was the Littleton's Arms, run by Benjamin Smith from 1797 at least, until his death in 1813. At 13 Snow Hill was the Vine. Thomas Martin

The Coach & Horses, Snow Hill, c. 1958.

is recorded as a licensed victualler here from 1822. He was followed by William Farmer in 1828. At 23 Snow Hill was the Chequers, run by Richard Kinnersley from 1767 to 1777.

The Coach & Horses at 30 Snow Hill was built around 1803. It was a narrow-fronted four-storey Georgian house, with a later added Victorian ground floor. It had a large central window with doors either side. The first recorded licensee of the Coach & Horses was Samuel Tolley, in 1818. For a period the house was known as the Lord Wellington, honouring the hero of Waterloo. By 1830 the house had been renamed the Coach & Horses. The Birmingham directories list the licensees that followed, including the magnificently named Benton Charles Dawes, there from 1875 to 1890. After his departure the Coach & Horses became an Ansells tied house. John Armitage saw in the twentieth century as landlord. In the post-Second World War period Snow Hill was blighted by future development, so there was a reluctance to spend money on houses like the Coach & Horses. In 1961 it and the other buildings this side of Snow Hill were demolished for the construction of the Inner Ring Road.

The Three Tuns, at 37 Snow Hill, originated at the start of the nineteenth century. Its first licensee was Joseph Hart, listed in the directory of 1803. The house was put up for auction on 15 September 1812. The details reveal:

> All that Freehold Messuage, three stories high, known by the name
> of the Three Tuns public house, in Snow Hill aforesaid, with Cellars,
> Brewhouse, Yard and Marble Alley, now in the occupation of Mr Hart.

The Tuns was sold for £420. Hart remained as licensee. His widow Martha continued to run the house until her own death in February 1826. William Thompson was landlord for over thirty-seven years, from 1849 to 1886. In 1888 licensee Ezekiel Wright called in architect William Jenkins to draw up plans for the modernisation of the house. It was completely revamped, updated and re-opened as the Manchester Hotel. There is an advertisement for the house in the *Birmingham Echo* for October 1913, when Bert Evans was licensee. The Manchester Hotel closed in the 1960s for the cutting of Snow Hill Queensway.

The Castle & Falcon was situated at the junction of Snow Hill and Slaney Street. Thomas Griffin was landlord from 1812 to 1823. He died at the ripe old age of eighty-one on 8 November 1836. The house was extensively modernised under licensee Thomas Poole in 1881-2, and thereafter advertised as a 'family and commercial hotel'. The City Brewery acquired the Castle & Falcon in late 1895, and the following year architect J.D. Wood was brought in to draw up plans for alterations and additions. The Castle & Falcon closed in 1909, when this section of Snow Hill was redeveloped with an arcade and shops.

The Barrel Inn at 50 Snow Hill was situated on the corner of Bath Street, on the edge of the old Gun Quarter. It functioned as a commercial centre for the gun trade, where 'Charge Men', having secured a large contract, would sub-let the contract to a number of local craftsmen. In the nineteenth century large profits were made by such men, who were given to drinking an unspecified drink called 'Colliers' Pop'. The Barrel originated in the early nineteenth century, George Perrin was its landlord in 1818. John Gayley appears in the trade directories as its licensee between 1827 and 1835. Over a forty-year period, 1840-86, the family of Bridgewater presided as licensees. Birmingham brewer William Butler acquired the house in 1893, and the following year rebuilt it to a design by architect William Jenkins. The house closed in 1903, while Arthur Wade Edge was landlord. A new three-storey house was built for M&B. It was Gothic in design, with gables and a clock tower above its main corner entrance. Four large lanterns projected from above the first floor; two on each street frontage. Charles 'Chalky'

ADVERTISEMENTS.

CASTLE & FALCON

COMMERCIAL HOTEL,

SNOW HILL,

OPPOSITE THE GT. WESTERN RAILWAY STATION,

BIRMINGHAM,

CHARLES GERBER,

PROPRIETOR.

EXCELLENT ACCOMMODATION.

Right: *An advertisement for the Castle & Falcon, Snow Hill.*

Below: *The Barrel Inn, corner of Snow Hill and Bath Street,* c. *1870.*

The Salutation Inn, Snow Hill, June 1961.

White, was its first landlord. The Crown fell victim to the Inner Ring Road of the late 1950s.

The Saracen's Head at 51 Snow Hill, was the first meeting place of the Birmingham Hampden Club, founded in 1812. This Radical organisation sought political reform by peaceful means. John Tayton was landlord then. Thomas Cheshire and later Job Martin followed him as licensees. Thomas Medlicott followed as the Saracen's Head's last landlord. The house closed in 1842. Seven doors down, and contemporary with the Saracen's Head, was the Warwick Arms. It was in existence by 1817, when John Slater was listed as licensee. For some thirty odd years, between 1825 and 1856, Joseph and Elizabeth Dunn ran the house. The Warwick Arms closed in 1898.

In or about 1775, the proprietor of the Golden Cross Inn, Mr Richard Ketley, founded the world's first building society. A plaque to this effect was presented to the City of Birmingham by the International Union of Building Societies and Saving & Loan Associations by its President, Mr Morton Bodfish, on 28 March 1958. Joseph Bates was landlord from 1817 to 1835. James Fox took over in 1875. He and his company retained control of the house until 1893, sub-leasing. Details of the layout of the house were described when its lease was offered for sale on 30 May 1890. It was described as :

An OLD LICENSED HOUSE, known as the GOLDEN CROSS, No.64, SNOW HILL, which contains two Bed Rooms and Closet, large Club Room, Spirit Room, Bar, Sitting Room, Kitchen, and three Cellars; and at the rear, approached by Side Entrance from the Street, is a Brewhouse (with Malt Room over), the usual Out-offices, and a large Range of Three-storey Shopping.

In its latter days the Golden Cross was let on an annual tenancy by Fox & Co., at a rent of £105 per annum. On 2 July 1891, James Fox being dead, the house was again put up for auction on a leasehold of thirteen years from Midsummer 1890. In the post-First World War period the Golden Cross was to know a further four licensees before its closure in 1927. George Jones was its last licensee.

Next door was the American Shades, opened in 1862 under Joseph E. Lee. In the following year the house is entered in the trade directory as the American Inn. Edward Pole was landlord in 1865. Later the house changed its name to the Wine & Spirit Vaults, but closed in 1867. At 73 Snow Hill was the curiously named Accommodation, established around 1838, with John Penny as its earliest recorded licensee. He was here until 1846, when John Tuckley took over from him. The house closed, was refurbished and updated, and re-opened as the Wheel. Tom Hodgetts is listed as its first licensee. The house apparently closed in 1872, there being no further directory entries.

The Salutation Inn, at 86 Snow Hill, was in existence by 1750, where it is shown on Bradford's Plan of Birmingham for that year. In the eighteenth century the Salutation was advertised:

> To be Lett, and entered upon at Midsummer next, a Good Messuage, known by the Name or Sign of the Salutation, at the Bottom of Snow Hill, Birmingham, with good Gardens, two Bowling Greens, and other Conveniences thereto belonging, now in the Tenure of Thomas Cotton. For particulars enquire of Mr John Kempson, of Birmingham Aforesaid.
>
> *Aris's Gazette*, 6 June 1763.

It was in a field just behind the Salutation, in 1798, that the last attempt at bull baiting in the town was thwarted. The Loyal Association, the local militia, marched on the pub and the mob dispersed, leaving the said bull. In 1817 James Cartwright took up the license. His son, William, and grandson Edward, followed him. Between them the family were landlords for over seventy years. The Salutation was rebuilt under Edward Cartwright's successor, Frederick Cook. He brought in well-known pub architect, William Jenkins (2 November 1887), to prepare drawings. In 1904 the Salutation was bought up by Holt Brewery of Aston, later taken over by Ansells, in 1934. During the 1960s the Salutation became a noted Trad Jazz pub, attracting local, national and international musicians. There was never any trouble at the Salutation, possibly due to the fact that downstairs behind the saloon bar was Alf 'Kid' Coates, featherweight runner-up in the Great Britain Championships of 1937. The Salutation was closed in 1968 and demolished soon after, perhaps unnecessarily, for the site remained undeveloped for fifteen years or more. Its last licensee was Gerry Keane, who later moved to the Anchor in Bradford Street.

Three more historical pubs remain. The Pitt's Head (named after Prime Minister William Pitt), was at 88 Snow Hill. It was in existence from *c.* 1765 to 1780. At 90 Snow Hill was the Indian Queen. Traditionally the name goes back to the seventeenth century, and commemorates Pocahontas (1595-1617). The pub is first recorded on 14 July 1789, when the lease was offered for sale at an auction held at the Hen & Chickens in the High Street. The licensee of the Indian Queen at the time was William Cox, who is first recorded there in 1785. Of the Blue Boar, at 104 Snow Hill, little is known, other than Ann Miller was listed as landlady from 1767 to 1774. Finally the White Swan at 130 Snow Hill. There is an obituary for one-time landlord, John Binns, in the *Birmingham Gazette* for 29 May 1820. It relates that he took over the Swan in 1811. The house apparently closed in 1850.

The post-Inner Ring Road pubs of the 1960s are also now gone. There was Fanny's, a mock Victorian tavern for Ansells, specialising in singsongs around the piano, and the Filibuster, another Ansells house, on two levels, later renamed the West End Bar. It was closed down by the police in December 2000.

The Gun Quarter

The ill-conceived Inner Ring Road of the 1960s tore through the old Gun Quarter. To make sense, the Quarter is treated as a whole entity. Steelhouse Lane, the southern boundary of the Quarter, took its name from Kettle's Steelhouses, erected here in the late seventeenth century. The Saracen's Head was offered for sale in 1812. In an advertisement in the *Birmingham Gazette* for 9 November, it is described as a 'capital public house and liquor shop in the midst of the gun and other extensive manufactories'.

Where once there were a dozen or more pubs, the Queen's Head is the only survivor in the street. It is the third house to bear this name. The first was popularly known as the Stamp, from the pub's sign above the doorway, depicting Queen Victoria's portrait from the Penny Black stamp. The house was built in the early eighteenth century, but did not become a pub until *c.* 1840. The pub was demolished in 1884 as part of the Improvement Scheme for the cutting of Corporation Street. The second of the three public houses of the same name was a narrow-fronted four-storey, red brick and terracotta establishment, built to the design of well-known pub architects James & Lister Lea, post January 1889. In the mid-1960s the second Queen's Head was closed down and demolished as part of the Inner Ring Road scheme. The third, and present, Queen's Head, an M&B house, was built in the mid-1960s, following the completion of the Inner Ring Road. It is a favourite lunchtime haunt of those working in the Inns of Court opposite, and journalists and staff of the Post & Mail.

The Dolphin, a beerhouse at 11 Steelhouse Lane, was also a casualty of the 1883 Improvement Scheme, as was the Punchbowl at No. 34. This house, down on the corner of Lancaster Street, was first licensed in 1817. John Gold was its first landlord. Charles Burbidge was licensee for thirty-four years, right up to the pub's closure. As well as a Queen's Head, there was also a King's Head, at 18 Steelhouse Lane. This pub dated from *c.* 1825, and closed in 1851. The Rose & Punchbowl closed about the same time. Situated at 55 Steelhouse Lane, it opened in 1840 with Elizabeth Hughes as its landlady.

Earlier eighteenth-century houses include the Cock, under Tom Gunn, listed in Sketchley's Directory of 1767, The Chequer, likewise listed in 1767 under licensee John Cooper, and the Bell at 59 Steelhouse Lane, in existence by 1767, with William Hawkesford as licensee. The house succumbed to the later Redevelopment Scheme of 1896, when the road was widened. The White Horse at No. 89 was a mid to late eighteenth-century house. William Collins ran the pub from 1790 until his death in September 1828. The house finally closed in 1870. Another victim of Victorian redevelopment was the Nelson at 99 Steelhouse Lane. Opened around 1820, it was situated on the corner of Russell Street, and disappeared with the building of the General Hospital.

Mrs Worrall, mistress of the Ship, at 70 Steelhouse Lane, died on 3 January 1819, as her brief obituary in the *Gazette* testifies. Her husband, Joseph, was landlord from 1810. Jane Brooke was here in 1887. With a closure notice served, she off-loaded the house on James Tabner. He was there for barely eighteen months before it closed.

The early Queen's Head, Steelhouse Lane, c. 1870.

The George & Dragon was at 134 Steelhouse Lane, on the corner with Weaman Street. In the Victorian era it brewed a rather strong ale called 'Dragon's Blood'. The house originated in the mid-eighteenth century, Thomas Hodson was listed as licensee in the trade directory of 1767. The house at the time was then known as the George. By 1790 its name had changed, and the house was kept by a Mr Whitehouse. A concert room was opened at the George & Dragon in 1825 under licensee Job Reeves, becoming what appears to have been the first music hall in Birmingham. A small platform served as a stage. The pub was later taken over by Reeves' sister and her husband, William Jones. In the spring of 1840, Louis Napoleon, later Napoleon III, visited the George & Dragon. It is believed that he was in Birmingham to purchase arms for his ill-fated attempt to secure the throne of France later that year. In 1858 the house was renovated under licensee, Mrs Millar. The Pheaseys took possession of the George and instigated 'Threepenny hops' on Saturdays and Mondays, at which customers might dance the night away. This old house closed in 1926, when Charles Hateley was landlord. It was demolished, and a new George & Dragon was built to the designs of James & Lister Lea. This house closed in 1960.

Left: *The present Queen's Head, the third on this site.*

Below: *The original George & Dragon, corner of Steelhouse Lane and Weaman Street.*

Of unknown location in Steelhouse Lane was the Royal Artillery Tavern. In 1800 the Birmingham Caledonian Society met here to celebrate St Andrew's Day, under landlord Hercules Hill. He was landlord here from 1798 to 1815. The Royal Hussar may perhaps have been its successor. It came into being in 1817, just after the Royal Artillery had closed. Other early nineteenth-century houses include the Freemasons' Tavern, of 1818, with Charles Machin as licensee, and the King's Arms, in existence under John Penny, 1822-28. Two more un-numbered houses; the Anchor, of 1767 with Samuel Mitchell as landlord, and the Victoria Arms, a beerhouse, for which architect O.P. Parsons drew up plans for modernisation on 26 August 1898. This establishment was one of four public houses in the neighbourhood of the Law Courts recommended for closure in 1917. The Turk's Head at 131 Steelhouse Lane had come into existence by 1828 under licensee, Samuel Leather. Alterations were carried out to the house by the architectural firm of Frewson & Cheadle for owners City Brewery Ltd, from plans drawn up on 7 September 1896. The Board at 94 Steelhouse Lane was established by 1848 with Elizabeth Williams listed as landlady; George Andrews had taken over by 1854. Charles Clayton took over in 1855; the house closed in the following year. At 109 Steelhouse Lane in the early nineteenth century was the Three Crowns, which dated from c. 1825. Francis Cook was licensee. His widow, Elizabeth, took over in 1838, remaining here until 1846. She was followed by William Dickin and later Charles Sharman. The Three Crowns closed in 1852.

Four more Steelhouse Lane pubs remain. The Coach & Horses, at 129, was situated on the corner of Slaney Street. It dated from 1783, when Thomas Postins was landlord,. Charles Hodson oversaw alterations to the house from his drawings of 26 January 1880. Further work was undertaken by architect Frederick Osborne in January 1893. The Gun, at 148, reflecting the quarter in which it was situated, was there, all but briefly, in 1869. The Gem Vaults at 148 Steelhouse Lane, are still remembered. They were situated on the northern side of the street, four doors down from Snow Hill. Though it had a narrow frontage onto the street, it was a long narrow pub, stretching back from the road to a depth of four rooms. The pub opened in 1854 under the partnership of Rawlins & Bridcut. Jonathan Green was put in as licensee. In 1867, while John Skelton was landlord, the house was entered in the trade directory as the Gem Wine & Spirits Vaults. In 1870 Sam Medlicott took over. He remained there until 1879. During his time the name was amended slightly to 'Stores'. This popular little town centre pub fell victim to the Inner Ring Road. The last of the known public houses in Steelhouse Lane was the Castle, at the junction of Steelhouse Lane and Corporation Street. It began life as the Castle Punchbowl in the early nineteenth century, at the junction with what was then Lichfield Street. During the cutting of Corporation Street, this beerhouse was demolished, but the license was retained. Plans were drawn up on 10 November 1885 for the construction of a new and much enlarged house. The new house was a four-storey edifice, given the full Victorian baronial treatment, topped off by mock battlements and towers. Inside it was the last word in luxury of the time. It had several bars, reflecting the social structure of the day, a snooker room and a committee room. The first licensee of the Castle was Frederick Wright, in 1886. He remained as landlord until his retirement in 1899. Thomas Harrison took over from him. In 1905 Charles Henry Green was appointed landlord. He was followed by Harry Barlow, Fred Hyde and Frank Bridges. During the 1930s and the post-war era, the Castle held snooker tournaments, graced by the likes of the great Joe Davis. The Castle survived the Second World War and the greyness of 1950s Birmingham. During the more egalitarian 1960s it still maintained a certain presence. It was closed for road improvements.

The Green Man, an Ansell's house on the corner of Sand Street, c. 1954.

A new arrival, at the junction of Steelhouse Lane and Corporation Street, was Fibber Magee's, an Irish theme pub opened by Northern Ireland Football International, Terry Neil, on 14 September 1995. It has since closed.

In Weaman Street was the curiously named Dog & Doublet, which is listed in the trade directory of 1767, with Thomas Coiny as licensee. The earliest recorded of the nineteenth-century pubs was the Lamp, specifically named in 1818, with Hannah Dutton as its landlady. As early as 1812, 'Mrs Dutton' was listed as a victualler here. The White Swan at 24 Weaman Street dated from 1817, when Mrs Mary Robinson was entered as its proprietor. In 1823, licensee Richard Cutler was also entered as a gun and pistol maker. The White Swan, an unassuming little backstreet local, was refused a renewal of license in 1917, and closed in the following year. George Parry put the towels on the pumps for the last time.

Three houses all opened by 1818 include the Marquis Cornwallis, The Golden Cross and the Leopard. The Marquis was named after General Charles Cornwallis (1738-1805). The house survived until 1903. The Golden Cross, whose first known licensee was William Young, closed in 1894. The Leopard, an 1818 house under John Ashford, was demolished in 1896. Later pubs along Weaman Street include the Cathedral, at 55, built c. 1840, taking its name from the nearby Roman Catholic Cathedral of St Chad; the Old Still at 73 Weaman Street, originating c. 1839 with Edward Davies as its first licensee, and closing in 1868; and the Rose & Crown at 71 Weaman Street, c. 1825 to 1904, George Blackwell being its last licensee. At 56 Weaman Street was the Nelson, opened in 1803 but renamed the Major Cartwright Arms in 1832 after John Cartwright (1740-1824), author and political reformer. It closed later that century. The Sir John Falstaff was in business about the same time. It originated in 1828 with William Bellamy as licensee. William Jenkins updated the pub from his plans of 7 February 1896. The house closed in 1922.

The Green Man on the corner of Weaman Street and 22 Sand Street dated from the early eighteenth century. In its latter years it was an Ansells house, tucked away in a quiet side street in the Gun Quarter. It was at one time home to the Musical Society, before its move to the White Hart in Digbeth. Its first known licensee in 1767 was Sarah Moore. The address of the house was given as 3 Weaman Street. By 1808 the address had changed to 22 Sand Street. In 1879, Arthur John Kett took over the license. He called in the firm of Looter & Latimer to update the Green Man. Legendry publican, Anthony Diamond, later of the Board in the Bull Ring, was landlord here between 1891 and 1894. With his departure the Green Man became an Ansells house. The quiet and unassuming Green Man was demolished post-1959 for the construction of the Post & Mail building.

Whittall Street runs parallel to Weaman Street. In 1893 the north-eastern side was completely removed for the building of the General Hospital, now the Childrens' Hospital. In its time though the street supported ten public houses. There was the Bull's Head, dating from 1808, the Plume of Feathers, under Charles Budd in 1800, the Eagle & Child, with Stephen Hill in 1818, the Coach & Horse, dating from 1818, under licensee William Siddons, and the Rose, a beerhouse which we know about because of an obituary of 4 April 1803 for landlord William Aston's wife.

At 17 Whittall Street was the Chapel Tavern, which took its name from the nearby chapel of St Mary on the Weaman Estate. It was a modest eighteenth-century house of three storeys, its first known licensee was Matthew Smith, listed in the 1818 directory. Thomas Palmer, who became landlord in 1851, was licensee for twenty-five years. His widow, Selina, took over in 1877 and called in architect Joseph Fidkin to draw up plans for its modernisation. The lease on the property expired in 1899 and the house was closed.

Left: *The Racquet Court Inn, Bath Street.*

Below: *The Bull, 41-42 Loveday Street.*

The Rose & Crown, originally at 14 Whittall Street, dated from *c.* 1798. William Aston was licensee between 1799 and 1818. He was followed by his son John, and between them they held the license for nearly sixty years. In 1878 a lady with the delightful name of Leolin Lampitt took over the house. This pub was one of three licensed victuallers recommended for closure in 1917. Its last licensee was Ambrose Joseph Flynn. Ten or so doors away was the Royal Exchange at No. 25. John Wiggins was the first licensee, from 1823 to 1850. Mary Henshaw was its last. The Exchange closed in 1902. The White House was a beerhouse, situated at 40 Whittall Street. Its licensee in 1865 was Charles Griffiths. The King's Arms, also at No. 40 but presumably there had been some street renumbering, dated from 1828, with Tom Swift as licensee. The house had a ninety-year life before the Licensing Justices withdrew its license in 1917. Sarah Jane Holyoak was its last licensee.

Slaney Street is now gone. It used to run alongside the old Gaumont Cinema in Colmore Circus, from Steelhouse Lane down to Snow Hill. It was named after Morton Slaney, an eighteenth-century attorney. There were three pubs along this narrow street. The Dog & Magpie, run by Henry and later William Morgan, between 1767 and 1777; The Royal Oak, a beerhouse at 17 Slaney Street, which was offered for sale in May 1875 and was described as having '…good Cellarage, Brewhouse, and Malt Room over…'; and The Cross Pistols was at 86, set back from the street, and approached down a narrow alleyway. The house had a low ceiling, and men above average height were obliged to stoop as they entered. The main room was very long, very low and only 6ft wide. Its fame rested upon the excellent quality of its home-brewed nut-brown ale. Sampson Dean, licensee up to 1805, has an obituary in the *Birmingham Gazette*. John Walker was landlord in 1818, when the house is first listed by name in the trade directory. After Walker, who died in 1823, came William Hand, William Amos, Alfred Durand and Samuel and Jane Parsons. The Cross Pistols closed in 1967.

The Gun, a beerhouse in Bath Street, took its name from the old Gun Quarter. It closed in 1927. The Turk's Head was at 32 Bath Street. It is listed as a public house in the trade directory of 1818, under landlord William Newey. In 1830 the house was taken over by William Brazenor and renamed the Welch Harper. The house, built *c.* 1805, was situated not far from the present St Chad's Cathedral. The Welch Harper closed in 1890.

The Racquet Court Inn in Bath Street was established *c.* 1747, and was noted as a venue for cockfighting. Later a purpose-built racquet court was established in the yard behind the pub. Among its leading exponents were J.B.A. Pereira and Thomas Henry Gem, who went on to formulate the rules of lawn tennis as we know them today. With the decline of racquets, the court was used for training boxers. Its then owner, 'Fence' Evans, taught heavyweight champion Bob Brettle how to box. The Racquet Court Inn and its former racquet court, were demolished in 1904. Still standing is the Gunmakers Arms at 92-93 Bath Street, on the corner with Shadwell Street. It dates from *c.* 1820. James Hill is its first recorded licensee. A Showell's Brewery tied house by 1896, improvements and alterations to the Gunmakers took place in 1890 to designs by architect A.H. Hamblin. The house was later taken over by Atkinson's of Aston, who were in turn taken over by M&B in 1958.

On the corner of 1 Price Street and 41-42 Loveday Street is the Bull's Head (known today simply as The Bull). It is claimed that this public house originated *c.* 1800. Certainly it can be dated from 1812, when Joseph Showell is listed as a victualler. Three generations of the Showell family, Joseph, Walter and Thomas, were licensees here in succession. They were followed by the Fulfords, who held the license over three generations too. The Bull's Head was bought up by Ansells and became a tied house. There was some doubt during the 1950s that it would survive the cutting of the notorious Inner Ring Road, but survive it did. Today it is a comfortable little pub that anyone would be pleased to call their local.

William Mole was landlord of the Black Horse at 51 Price Street in 1818. He was listed as a victualler here as early as 1808. Mole and his wife, Mary, ran this pub until post-1830. This house survived the First World War, closing in 1920. The last known public house in Price Street, the Frighted Horse, run by Mary Mole from 1828-30, is probably an alternative name for the Black Horse. In Loveday Street, at No. 34, was the Dog & Partridge, a beerhouse, later taken over by Frederick Smith's Aston Model Brewery and re-licensed as a full public house. It closed in 1937. At 75 Loveday Street was The Dog, first listed by name in Pigot's Directory of Birmingham for 1828. Mary Adcock was its licensee from 1823 to 1842. Her daughter Ann served as landlady until 1852. The Jones family, John and Eliza, ran the house for fourteen years, their tenure cut short in 1892. The Dog was demolished for the building of the General Hospital. The Argyle at No. 19 opened in 1864 under licensee Samuel Burn. Thereafter there are no further references to this house. At 49 Loveday Street was the Cold Bath, its name harking back to a stream that ran near here. Its license was surrendered in 1883 under the Improvement Scheme. Finally there was the Nelson at 17 Loveday Street, established by button maker John Greenway, c. 1821. His widow took over the premises in 1828. The house was closed in 1881 when this part of the street was cleared for the extension of Corporation Street.

Princip Street takes its name from the Princip family who were landowners here from the mid-eighteenth century. At No. 2 was the Glasscutters' Arms, a beerhouse, dating from 1865 with J.P. Grimley as licensee. There was another beerhouse at 19, the Britannia, whose name comes to light at its closure in 1938. The Coachsmith's Arms, a third beerhouse, was advertised for sale by auction in August 1887. The Malt Shovel was at 21 Princip Street. There is an obituary for its first licensee, Thomas Allen, in the *Gazette* for 7 February 1842. By 1853 the house was known as the Old Malt Shovel. It closed in 1877. Finally there was the Fox & Dogs at 63 Princip Street. In 1882 William Joseph Whittall drew up plans for landlord William Chambers for alterations to bring the house up to date. The Fox & Dogs closed in 1909.

Stafford Street to Moor Street

There was a grouping of little streets just off Steelhouse Lane; some have gone, others were renamed and some were truncated during the upheavals of the 1960s. London Prentice Street (later renamed Dalton Street), had a number of licensed establishments. The Bell at 36 London Prentice Street was in existence in 1862, under landlord Joshua Caldwell. The Lincoln Inn was in Dalton Street in 1891. Alterations were made under the direction of architect Henry Hendricks. The Lamp was at 16 London Prentice Street from 1767 to 1777, under licensee John Barker. The London Apprentice, in 1755, displayed the 'Modern Living Colossus'. He was featured in *Aris's Gazette* for 4 May 1752, complete with a woodcut depicting the young man:

> This is to acquaint the Curious, That there is coming to this town Mr Blaker, the modern Living Colossus, or Wonderful Giant, who has given such universal satisfaction in London, will be seen at the London Apprentice, in Birmingham, at the Fair and for some Time after.

Curiously the giant's height is not given.

The Old King's Arms was at 14-15 London Prentice Street. It is listed in the directories from 1818 under licensee William Taylor. The house was abandoned in 1883 under the Improvement Scheme. The Anchor was situated on the corner of Dalton Street and Newton Street and dated

The Hope & Anchor, a notorious nineteenth-century beerhouse.

from 1812, with John Price as its first known licensee. A licensed victuallers, it closed in early 1918. Of the replacements for these departed houses there has been but one, the Ansells house the Costermonger, situated at the junction of the truncated Dalton Street and Lower Bull Street, known as Dalton Way. Steps lead down to a large darkened room, frequented by a young Gothic element that enjoy Heavy Metal.

At Tanter Street, later renamed Ryder Street, were two pubs, the Roebuck and the Nelson. At 22 Tanter Street, alternatively known briefly as Anthony Street, was the Roebuck, dating from *c.* 1767. It was run by Nathaniel Meecham, and later his son, David. William Brown was landlord in 1776, when the house was renumbered. Thereafter it appears to have closed. The Nelson originated pre-1818 under licensee John Archer. Its license was temporarily surrendered under the Improvement Scheme, but was later restored. In 1892 the address was changed to 68 Ryder Street. The Lord Nelson, as it is then listed, closed in 1898. The Bell was in James Watt Street, now James Watt Queensway, near Aston University. Additions were made to the establishment in 1891 from plans drawn up by Samuel Taylor. The Hope & Anchor, a beerhouse, and consequently not recorded by name in the trade directories, was situated on the corner of the Gullet and Stafford Street. Situated in an unsavoury part of the town, it was demolished at the time of the Improvement Scheme and the cutting of Corporation Street. During the time of its last licensee, Henry Allwood, and no doubt a long time before, it staged dog fights and ratting matches. The rat pit in the yard at the rear was described as 'an octagonal structure about four feet across, with wooden floor. The sides consisted of vertical or unclimbable iron bars, which rose to a height of about three feet.'

Stafford Street, the old road to the north, supported at least eight known public, or beerhouses. In 1767, Joseph Little was landlord of the Lamp, and Ann Hammond was landlady of the nearby Rose. At the Bull's Head at the same time was Benjamin Kelsey, landlord until 1777. John Dafforn was licensee at the Golden Ball at 13 Stafford Street between 1767 and 1777. There was also a beerhouse at No. 36, the Stag's Head, which surrendered its license in 1883. There were three houses on the corner of Stafford Street and Tanter (or Ryder) Street. The Barley Mow, at 23 Stafford Street, was on the corner of 1 Tanter Street. The first known publican was Joseph Greaves, landlord from 1817 to post-1824. John Jackson and his widow, Ann, followed. They ran the house for thirty years. It eventually closed in 1898, Theophilius Pare was its last licensee. The Golden Cup, its address also given as 23 Stafford Street, appears to have been on the opposite side of the street. It originated about 1828 with John Sharp as its first landlord. Edward Sills and his wife ran the Cup from c. 1830 to 1863. The license was temporarily abandoned in 1883, but restored later that year. Thomas Lancaster was licensee when the house temporarily closed in 1892. It was rebuilt, and re-opened that same year as a three-storied public house with an octagonal corner tower, designed by architect Matthew J. Butcher, and renamed the Victoria. It closed, and was demolished for the cutting of the Stafford Street section of the Inner Ring Road during the early 1960s.

Moor Street

Moor Street is one of the city's oldest streets. It was originally called Mole Street, a corruption of 'molendum', a mill. There was a water mill here until the end of the seventeenth century. Turning the corner from the Bull Ring, on the right-hand side of Moor Street was the Outrigger, an Ansells house built after the completion of Moor Street Queensway. It was a curious building on stilts, erected over the entrance to St Martin's car park. Décor wise it had a nautical feel, with a Bilge Bar downstairs and a Gun deck quarter upstairs. It was demolished in preparation for the Millennium redevelopment of the Bull Ring. Its predecessor, more or less on the same site, was the Tamworth Arms, at 5 Moor Street. It dated from 1822, with James Smith as its first licensee. Prominent pub architect William Jenkins carried out alterations and updating to the inn, including a new frontage, from plans drawn up on 2 October 1890. The Tamworth Arms narrowly survived the Blitz of 1941, but fell to the Birmingham planners. It was demolished in 1958 for the cutting of the Inner Ring Road.

The Fleur de Lys, at what was later to become 4 Moor Street, is believed to have been sixteenth century in origin. Legend has it that part of the Fleur was incorporated into the later Woolpack next door, but certainly in the late eighteenth century it still existed as a separate entity. John Eades is listed as landlord from 1767 to 1774, and after him was Francis Eades, presumably his son. In 1800 the Fleur de Lys was pulled down for the building of the Public Office, forerunner of the Council House. As a public house, the Woolpack next door could trace its origins as a building back to 1340. During the sixteenth century it was the home of William Lench, a great benefactor to the poor of the town. The earliest authenticated record of this house as a tavern is dated 1709, when the 'Wooll Packe' was in the hands of John Ensor. The new house absorbed two older houses, the Green Tree and the Fleur de Lys. Dr Samuel Johnson, compiler of the first dictionary,

The Outrigger, Moor Street.

The Roebuck, Moor Street, the building on the extreme right.

The Aquarium, Moor Street.

was a frequent visitor at the Woolpack, as was the printer John Baskerville. In October 1819, Sir Rowland Hill, of penny post fame, established the Society for Literary Improvement here. In the latter part of the nineteenth century the Woolpack became a cricketing pub, and was the headquarters of the 'Gentlemen Players' of England. With the opening of the Public Office next door it became the haunt of magistrates, barristers, solicitors and town councillors. In February 1885 some 15ft of the inn, fronting onto Moor Street, was demolished when the new building line of the street was established. A new frontage was constructed and major refurbishment was carried out to the house from plans drawn up by architect W.H. Ward on 14 January 1885. The redeveloped house re-opened as the Woolpack Hotel. This famous old pub was demolished in 1958 for the cutting of the insidious Inner Ring Road.

At 32 Moor Street was the Roebuck, just four doors up from the old Public Office. It was probably late seventeenth century in origin, but altered in the Georgian period. It had a central doorway, with two square projecting windows either side. Above the doorway was a large globe lantern. Thomas Hollowell was landlord in 1767, the 'Widow Holliwell' was licensee in 1774. A bottle store was added, and other alterations were made by noted pub architects James & Lister Lea from plans submitted on 2 March 1888. Yet despite its modernisation the Roebuck lasted barely seven more years; it closed in 1895.

The White Lion was an old timber-framed public house dating back to Tudor times. The earliest verifiable licensee was a 'Mr Guest', who died on 16 October 1765. Thomas Guest, who appears to be his son, is listed as licensee in 1767. He was followed by Robert Squire, Edward Morris, Thomas Newman, and the White Lion's last landlord, Thomas Cooper. The old house

Dingley's Hotel, Moor Street, July 1933.

closed in 1835. At 34 Moor Street was the Crown, listed in the directories from 1823 to 1839. Four doors up at 38 was the Rose, which was apparently a beerhouse. Joseph Carter whose death is recorded in the *Gazette*, was landlord from 1770 to 15 July 1780. Then there was the Rose & Crown at No. 38. It was in existence from 1767 up to its eventual closure in 1924. Joseph Carter was its first licensee, and William Henson its last. The Mitre was at 40 Moor Street, and originated prior to 1818. It was a licensed victuallers, eventually closing in 1897. The White Horse was established by 1780. There is a reference to the house being a recruiting pub for the Warwickshire Militia in *Aris's Gazette* for 4 November 1791. Sergeant Pring was the recruiting sergeant. An old beerhouse, in 1951 Charles Gammidge belatedly purchased a full license from the Justices for £2,000. The house was closed in 1958 for the construction of the Inner Ring Road.

The Green Man, whose first known licensee was Richard Blackford, was situated at 54 Moor Street. It closed in 1843. A very short-lived house was the Cup at 65. William Yates was landlord in 1860. At 67 was the Boot & Bottle, established by 1818 under licensee William Jones. It closed post-1842. The Lion, operating from 1767 to 1776 under George Muddiman and later James Wakeman, was at No. 77.

The Aquarium in Moor Street was a licensed victuallers with just that little bit extra to attract customers. It had an elaborate frieze around the bar depicting fish, eels and other sea creatures. Needless to say it specialised in seafood. Jabez White, a noted local bare-knuckle boxer, kept the house in the late nineteenth century. The Aquarium closed in 1924.

At 85 Moor Street was the Crown & Pensioner. There in 1828, its only known licensee was William Foxall. Thomas Medlicott took the house over, post-1828, and renamed it the Bull's Head. In all it had five further licensees before its closure in 1879. The Carriers' Arms, a beerhouse, was at 89 Moor Street. John Cooper was its landlord in 1869.

On the other side of the road, at the junction of Moor Street and New Meeting Street, was Dingley's Hotel. It was a licensed victuallers, which began life as The Board under landlady Mary Ann Dingley. Soon known by the name of its proprietor, the name remained after her death, right up to the closure of the house in the 1960s, for the cutting of the Inner Ring Road. One of its more colourful owners was John Millward, who it was said dined each day off silver dishes. He had a perverse nature. It was said that he would keep the house empty rather than admit a guest of whom he disapproved. On one of the corner tables were some teeth marks, made by a strongman who was appearing at one of the Birmingham music halls. As a demonstration of his strength he took hold of this table by his teeth and lifted it off the ground, allegedly fully laden. This lovely old hotel with public bar was swept away for the Ring Road.

The Corner was opened in 1927 under licensee William Henson. He was followed in 1930 by John James D'Arcy. Arthur Parker was landlord after him. Arthur Hardy and Bill Fisher were licensees during the 1940s. The house was closed in the late 1950s for the construction of Moor Street Queensway. Its license was transferred to the Wandering Minstrel in the Bull Ring Shopping Centre, which opened on 27 May 1964. The Great Western, at 138 Moor Street, took its name from the nearby railway station. This was a beerhouse that opened in 1869. The Great Western closed in 1939. At 147 was the Ship, dating from 1767. Francis Miles was its landlord up to 1774. The Struggler Alive – a curiosity in more ways than one. The name seems unique to English pub names. It is referred to in the trade directory of 1855, but no licensee was given. At 149 Moor Street was the Justice Tavern, an old beerhouse situated next door to the Waterloo Tavern, and three doors up from the Beehive Inn at No. 152. It was in existence by 1865 under licensee R. Broomhall, and it is known that alterations were made

MUNICH
LAGER BIER

ON DRAUGHT

AT

"The Continental,"

149, MOOR ST.,

. . . # BIRMINGHAM.

—:o:—

CONTINENTAL DELICACIES.

THE BEST VALUE ALWAYS APPRECIATED.

The Continental, Moor Street, specialised in German beer.

to the house from plans drawn up by Joseph Hidkin on 18 June 1878. The Waterloo Tavern, previously mentioned, began life as the Lisbon Wine Vaults in 1861 under licensee William Goodman. It became the Waterloo in 1865, fifty years after the famous battle. Enoch Palmer was its first landlord.

The Continental, at 149 Moor Street, was known for its continental beers, as its name suggests, and in particular its 'Munich Lager Bier'. There is an advertisement for the establishment in the *Birmingham Echo*, 11 October 1913. Briefly, there remain some beerhouses to list.; the Blue Pig, in existence from 1819 to 1841, The White Swan, with landlord, William Bagnall, 1767. Also in 1767 was the Lamp, with Benjamin May. The Royal Oak was run by Henry Murrant, 1767 to 1777, and the General Elliott, which in 1792, under landlord, Henry Biggs, issued a halfpenny token.

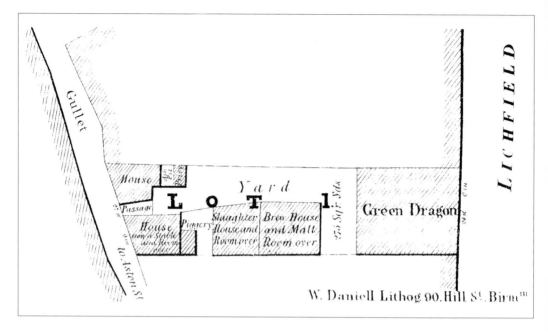

The Green Dragon, a well-regulated house with a slaughterhouse combined.

Corporation Street and Roads Leading Off

Lichfield Street, a thoroughfare replaced by the present Corporation Street, formed the spinal road of the early eighteenth-century development known as the Priory Estate. It was developed from *c.* 1710, but it is not until 1767 that we get details of public, and beerhouses, situated here. One such was the Lamp Tavern, an establishment of 1767-1777, run by Charles Friend. Of this same period was the Mermaid, run by William Bridgens. At the Golden Acorn, at that same time, was John Hill, and at the Golden Ball was landlady Rachel Dent. These, and the five following licensed premises, do not have street numbers, so it is difficult to say with any certainty whether at the end of their directory entries they closed, or were renamed. The Coach & Horses is recorded in 1818, with William Wheeler as landlord, Thomas Southam was running the Swan in 1817-18. The Golden Lion was a beerhouse, which comes to our notice with the death in 1807 of the wife of its landlord, John Ball. The Cup's 1810 landlord is known only as 'White'. Finally there was the Royal Oak, open *c.* 1837 to 1866. Numbered houses along Lichfield Street include The Cock, at No. 8, with Elizabeth Parsons as landlady in 1840-41. A little earlier in 1828 was the Anchor with Matthew Kelly, at 18 Lichfield Street, which appears to have evolved into the Acorn, under the same Matthew Kelly. It closed in 1871 for the cutting of Corporation Street. The Sportsman was at 22, with John Smallwood as licensee in 1861. At 34 was the Bull's Head, an 1850s house under Richard Busst. Ten doors up was the Turk's Head at 44, a beerhouse originating *c.* 1875 under licensee, Henry Getley. Its license was surrendered in 1882 under the Improvement Scheme. At 47 was the Heart & Hand, originally known as the Hand & Heart. This public house dated from the 1830s, with William Reader listed as licensee. The license was abandoned in 1880. The Green Dragon was at 52 Lichfield Street. When offered for sale on 16 April 1839 it was advertised as:

All that well-accustomed and commodious licensed PUBLIC HOUSE and Premises, known by the Name of 'THE GREEN DRAGON,' situated fronting to Lichfield-street, consisting of six good Chambers, large Club Room, extending the entire length of the Front, Parlour, Bar, Tap Room, extensive Cellering under the whole, Brewhouse, and Malt Room, Pump, Yard, &c. with Cow House, Slaughter-house and other Buildings at the Back.

The first known entry for the house is in the Directory of Birmingham for 1812, where Edward Millward was listed as landlord. During the 1860s the house was run by John Taberner. The last licensee of the Green Dragon was Annie Perry. The license of the house was transferred to the Court Restaurant in 1883.

The Star was one of the earlier public houses along Lichfield Street, dating from 1767, with John Chambers as licensee. It was on the corner of Newton Street, and had, according to an advertisement in the *Gazette* (14 April 1806), 'four lodging rooms and stabling for four horses'. The license to this house was surrendered in 1883 and transferred to the Central Restaurant in Cannon Street. The Odd Fellows' Arms at 57, opened in 1855 with Mrs Louisa Pennell as its first licensee. The house closed in the 1880s for the cutting of Corporation Street. The Hog in Armour (a rather surreal name for a pub), was in existence by 1785, when maltster and victualler William Edwards was in charge. His obituary is recorded in the *Gazette* during October 1791. At 79 Lichfield Street was the King's Head, in existence between 1823 and 1830, under William Gibson. The Hand & Shears at 84, had two licensees between 1767 and the house's apparent closure in 1770, William Claybrooke and William Edwards. The license of the Shamrock Tavern, reflecting that this was once part of the Irish Quarter, was surrendered in 1882 under the Improvement Scheme. The White Lion was originally at 47 Lichfield Street. Dating from *c.* 1817, it closed in 1830. Right next door was the Rose & Crown, a fairly unassuming early eighteenth-century two-and-a-half-storey house with attic windows in the roof space. The house was photographed in 1883 as part of the Improvement Scheme Survey. Condemned to demolition, its license was abandoned in 1886.

The Nag's Head at 116 Lichfield Street was in existence by 1818. The licensee was Thomas Westwood. In its last years this house was kept by his son, Thomas (II), whose son, John, went on to take up the license of the Woodman in Easy Row. In Local Notes & Queries (1165), 'Father Frank' described Thomas (II): 'He was a perfect gentleman of the old school, regular in his habits, straight as a pikestaff, and dressed as neatly and carefully as a clergyman.' Of the pub itself he continues:

> The Nag's Head parlour was a select sanctum, into which no stranger was expected to pass unless he was introduced by one of the habitués. Each gentleman sat in a certain chair; and above many of the walls was the portrait of the gentleman sitting underneath. I remember, on one of my casual visits, noticing a gentleman enter the room, and fidget from chair to chair. I could not explain to myself why he was so unsettled, till my next door neighbour whispered in my ear, 'that I was occupying that gentleman's chair'. I arose with alacrity, and though the old fellow bade me not disturb myself, I saw that he was glad when he had got his right seat. 'For you see, I have only missed sitting in this chair once in thirty-five years, and that was one Christmas night when there was deep snow, and my wife would not let me come out for fear of accidents.'

The license of the Nag's Head was abandoned in 1879 under the Improvement Scheme.

The entrance of the Crown, Corporation Street.

The last of the pubs was the Old Farriers Arms at 122 Lichfield Street. Architecturally the only thing that distinguished it from its neighbours was the old square lantern above the door. As a pub it dated from 1834. George Jones was its first landlord. He remained as licensee for twenty years or more, being followed by his son, Harry Jones, in 1855. The license was surrendered in 1883 as part of the Improvement Scheme for the cutting of Corporation Street.

Corporation Street cut through some of the worst slums in central Birmingham. Begun in August 1878, it was not until 1903 that the road linking New Street with Aston Street was complete. In the process all of the above public houses were swept away. Of their replacements there were but few. The most outstanding must be the Crown, at 182 Corporation Street. Formerly known as the George & Crown, and dating back to 1823, it was demolished for the cutting of Corporation Street. The site was acquired by William Butler's Crown Brewery of Broad Street, on a seventy-five-year lease at an annual rent of £500. The house he had built was later updated following the merger of Butler with Henry Mitchell to form M&B. Architect Charles J. Hodson drew up plans on 4 January 1888. His building, on two levels, is in the style of the French Second Empire, with tall canted bays, Inside it has an impressive twenty-foot high ceiling. On 21 October 1930, M&B managed to buy the freehold of the building, known as Court Chambers, and with it the three floors above, comprising offices and showrooms. The clientele of the Crown are mainly lawyers, police, and of course the people that bring them together in court; all rubbing shoulders together amicably.

Yates' Wine Lodge, now gone, was an institution – it was an experience, the last refuge of the South African wine drinker and other odd characters banned from most other pubs. Yet there was never any trouble. It had a sign, 'Silence is Golden: customers are regrettably requested not to raise their voices unduly in conversation.' And they did not. The premises ran through from Corporation Street to Cannon Street, with access from both streets, up or down flights of stairs. There was a huge upstairs lounge, its ceiling 25ft high, with huge rotor-bladed fans suspended from the ceiling. The lower bar, approached down a flight of stairs, had tubular railings regulating the approach to the bar, and the traditional cast-iron round tables – found in most 1960s pubs at the time – had a small brass rail about them too. They were the type of tables seen on ships, the rail preventing the glasses sliding off in heavy swells. Most strange, given Birmingham's distance from the sea. South African wine was popular here, though the establishment did in its closing years sell beer and cider. In April 1977, Yates', the Lancashire-based company, announced the closure of its Birmingham branch. Some thirteen years later, in June 1990, with a more upmarket image, a new Yates' was opened in a rather splendid old Victorian building near the old Law Courts. The Marshall Foch, at 184 Corporation Street, opened in 1918 under licensee Robert Oxley. It was named after the French Commander in Chief of the Allied Armies, Marshall Ferdinand Foch (1851-1929). In 1930, the house closed.

The Square Peg at 115 Corporation Street, a Weatherspoon's pub, opened in part of the old Lewis's department store in January 1995. The site cost £1.2 million to convert. In area the pub is 6,000 square feet; it is approximately six times the size of an average pub.

RSVP, a Whitbread Brewery house situated on the corner of the Old Square, was (it was claimed) the largest pub in the city, with a capacity for 900 customers. Not perhaps as large as the 1960s Swan at Yardley, but then again the Swan was a good example of what is biggest is not always best. RSVP opened on 23 October 1999 at a cost of £1.2 million. The premises failed to attract the requisite 900 customers, and is now a Tesco's.

Leading off from Lichfield Street (the present Corporation Street) between the Old Square and Lancaster Circus, were four little streets: Thomas Street, St John Street, Newton Street and the Priories. The first known licensee of the mid-eighteenth-century Brickmaker's Arms in

The King of Prussia, a drawing by Paul Braddon.

Thomas Street was Thomas Barber, a brick maker, hence its name, and was most probably the builder of this public house. The White Swan was a beerhouse, first recorded in 1817 with John Turner as licensee. It closed in the 1870s as part of the Improvement Scheme. The Three Tuns had Stephen Salt as licensee from 1808 to 1818. Tamar Ingram took over from him and was landlord until post-1830. The Hope & Anchor at 1 and 2 Thomas Street was on the corner of Lichfield Street. The license was abandoned in 1883. At No. 3 was the Red Bull, originating in 1834, and in 1861, under Con O'Callaghan, was renamed the Rose. It closed in 1883. At 16 Thomas Street was the Liverpool Tavern. Elizabeth Gunn was landlady in 1829. In 1840 it became the Jolly Bacchus under Joseph Timmings. It too closed in 1883, under the Improvement Scheme.

The Malt Shovel at 22 Thomas Street dated from 1807. Its first licensee, Thomas Clewley, was there until 1829. The house was situated on the corner of Dale End. The Royal Oak, on the other side of the street, was in existence by 1817, but had closed by 1845. A few doors up, but a century earlier, was the Gun, run by Harry Bond and his son, William, between 1767 and 1770. Un-numbered were the Blue Boar, a beerhouse under Henry Griffiths, 1818-20, The Red Lion of 1767, with John Harris, and the Crown, situated on the corner of Tanter Street, in 1803.

In John Street there were at least seven public houses. There was the Lamb & Flag at No. 12, dating from 1818 (closed in 1886), the Lion & Lamb at 39, in existence in 1855, and the Horse & Groom at 42 John Street, which opened pre-1823. Un-numbered public houses here include the Cutler's Arms of 1767-1777, the Anchor, c. 1773, closing in 1883, and the (Old) Crown, dating from 1774, with Adam Snape as licensee, which closed around 1818.

Newton Street, dating from the early eighteenth century, was named after Quaker Stephen Newton. Early pubs here, now all gone, included the Steam Coach Tavern, dating from 1833, named after Heaton's steam carriage of 1833; the Golden Boy of 1767; the Plumber's Arms at 12 Newton Street, from 1823 to 1867; and the Freemasons Arms at 6 Newton Street, run by John and his wife Ann Free from 1785 to 1820. The license of the Plough & Harrow, at 31 Newton Street, was abandoned in 1880 under the Improvement Scheme.

There were three licensed victuallers in Newton Street, two of whom were closed by the Justices in 1917 as part of their 'fewer but better' scheme: the Crown at 23, popular with off-duty policemen and those working at the Law Courts, and the Belgian Arms, again situated near the courts. The Horse & Groom was closed in May 1922.

The King of Prussia, 16 Newtown Street, was named after Frederick the Great, who, having allied himself with England against France in 1756, became a popular hero. This may indicate when the pub was granted its license. There is an obituary for one-time licensee, Jacob Godwin, who died at the house on 5 December 1816. He had been landlord of the King of Prussia since 1805. The license of this pub, then a Trent Brewery tied house, was abandoned temporarily in 1883 under the Improvement Scheme. The house re-opened under licensee Mrs Emma Heaton, but closed in 1918.

Lower Priory runs from Dale End to the Old Square, and Upper Priory from the Square up to Steelhouse Lane. At 3 Lower Priory was The Stores, a beerhouse of unknown age. In 1883 it was obliged to surrender its license for the construction of Corporation Street. Following completion, the license was renewed. It finally closed in January 1907. The Lion at 21 was another beerhouse. It too surrendered its licence in the 1880s, but was then demolished. The Board, a nineteenth-century licensed victuallers in Lower Priory, closed in the 1960s for the construction of the Inner Ring Road. At 16 Lower Priory was the Waterloo Tavern, which opening in 1815, and which commemorated Wellington's great victory of that year. Ambrose Dee was its first licensee. He was followed by six more licensees before the arrival of Joseph Wilkins, its long-time landlord. He was obliged to surrender the license in 1883, under the Improvement Scheme. The license was restored, and prestigious architects Martin & Chamberlain, better known for their Board Schools, were called in to design a new house in 1886. The Tavern continued as a public house until October 1902, when the Old Square and its environs were redeveloped. The focus of the Old Square was the Stork Inn, dating from 1816. The house closed in 1883, when Corporation Street was driven through this early eighteenth-century square. On the other side of the Square was the Private & Commercial Hotel, with a public bar. It opened under the Misses J. & H. Allen in 1849. It became Tainsh's Hotel, and like the Stork it was swept away with the 1883 redevelopments. The only replacement in the Square was the Cabin. It opened on 26 October 1966. The Cabin was renamed the Priory in 1994, and followed further refurbishment, has become a pub-cum-nightclub known as B3, reflecting its postcode.

Onto Upper Priory, here there were three public houses. The Freemasons' Arms was at 27 Upper Priory. John Morgan was its first known licensee. He was there from 1790 up to his death on 10 April 1797. The house was temporarily closed in 1856, extensively updated, and re-opened as the White Swan under Harry Reynolds in the following year. It closed for the cutting of Corporation Street. Next door at 28 was the Golden Cup, in existence by 1767, with Joseph

Green as licensee. It closed *c.* 1835. Finally there was the Bull's Head at No. 14, originating *c.* 1780 under the 'Widow Boole'. Thomas Foxall was landlord in 1818 when the Bull's Head was also listed as a Tripe House. The pub was demolished in 1883 for the construction of Corporation Street, but when this was completed, a new house was built, based upon drawings prepared on 10 May 1882, by Thomas Gray. The new Bull's Head was closed in June 1959 for the cutting of Priory Queensway.

New Street

New Street, despite is name, dates back to 1379. The King's Head was situated almost opposite the second Hen & Chickens, previously mentioned. It was in its upper room, in 1774, that the Birmingham Assay Office was first established. When the old timber-framed house was eventually pulled down, the inn sign was acquired by the Assay Office, and now hangs in their Newhall Street premises. The Crown, situated opposite the old grammar school, was set back slightly from the road behind a horse trough. John Cottrell, a saddler, owned it in 1704. He left it to his son in his will of that year. Next door to the Crown was the Wheatsheaf. On its inn sign was painted a sheaf of wheat standing in a field, and behind it was a roadside public house, the sign of which was the Barley Mow. This naturally led to some confusion, and this public house was known as the Wheatsheaf by some, and the Barley Mow by others. Its landlord in 1767 was Henry Read. In 1800 its new landlord, Edward Pugh, operated a coach service running from Birmingham to Leamington, via Warwick. It was patronised by the elderly and those of a nervous disposition. Pugh also kept a funeral hearse, and this may perhaps explain why he reputedly drove so slowly. The Wheatsheaf closed in 1833.

St James Tavern (Jimmy's), New Street.

Above: *The Waterloo Tavern, Lower Priory, c. 1870.*

Left: *A plan of 1870 showing the Waterloo Tavern and the Stork Hotel.*

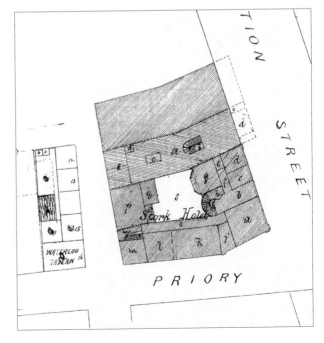

CHRIST CHURCH PASSAGE BIRMINGHAM.

SEMPER IDEM

WATERLOO BAR

THE WATERLOO BAR,
CHRIST CHURCH PASSAGE,
BIRMINGHAM.

The Suite of rooms comprising the Waterloo Bar are the most complete and unique of their class in the Country.

COLD LUNCHEONS, CHOPS, STEAKS, SOUPS, &c.

Above: *An advertisement for the Waterloo Bar, New Street.*

Left: *The popular George Hardy, licensee of the Waterloo, 1908.*

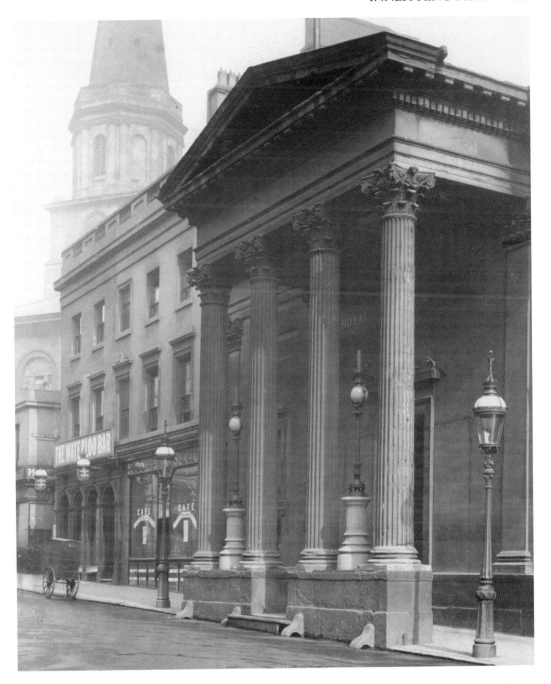

The RBSA Gallery, and beyond it the Waterloo Bar, c. 1895.

Above left: *A political cartoon, featuring Joseph Chamberlain and Joe Hillman.*

Above right: *An appreciation of Hillman's Stores, from the Dart, June 1887.*

Opposite: *An advertisement for Hillman's Stores.*

Jimmy's, a fashionable 1950s bar in New Street, began life as a licensed victuallers, under William Ehrentraut, having evolved out of the late nineteenth-century St James' Luncheon Store. By the 1930s the establishment, mainly used by professional people, was described in the trade directories as a restaurant with public bar. Jimmy's, situated at 120 New Street, closed in 1965. A few doors away at 117 New Street was the Commercial Hotel, originating in 1847. It closed in 1855. The Green Man, situated on the corner of Needless Alley, was an early Victorian beerhouse; it closed *c.* 1870. At 137 New Street was Walters' Swan Hotel, which opened in 1853 under licensee Mrs Mary Walters. The delightfully named Wignall Avison was licensee in 1863. In 1891 the Hotel was taken over by the Wolverhampton Star & Garter Hotel Co., who ran it until its closure in 1906. Almost at the top of New Street, some sixty-six years later, was the popular Bogart's Bier Keller. It opened in 1972 under licensee John Stokes. It sold Munich-brewed Lowenbrau, served up in stone steins. Bogart's, with its live music, discotheque and games room, was a magnet to the young. Just 450 people were allowed in under its license, but 700 customers at a time was not uncommon. Bogart's became a victim of its own success. Its overcrowding led to reproaches from the Licensing Justices, who eventually refused to renew its license. Following an unsuccessful appeal, Bogart's was closed in June 1981.

JOE HILLMAN'S,

A Favourite Birmingham Haunt, soon to be removed to make way for the New Post Office.

Isis, formerly the Royal Mail, from Pinfold Street.

The Waterloo Bar was a popular Victorian eating house. It had its heyday under George Hardy, a man who did not suffer fools gladly. There was a story told of how an Anglican minister who dined there regularly requested that the chicken leg he had received should be exchanged for a wing. Hardy retorted that the minister should be informed that 'God made fowl to walk as well as fly, and if he [the minister] knows a bird with four wings and no legs, I'll take the lot.' The clergyman ate his chicken leg. Hardy took up the lease of the premises in 1876 from a Miss Robinson. At the time it was a small eating house. He saw the potential, particularly in its positioning close to the General Post Office and the Council House. Board School architects Martin & Chamberlain in 1880 and William Wykes in 1887 extensively renovated the premises. A bar was fitted out, the grill room furnished substantially and a smoke room was made as cosy and comfortable as possible. It speedily became one of the most popular bars in the town. In 1894 the block of buildings in which the Waterloo Bar was situated was put up for sale. The premises were acquired by the Birmingham Hotel & Restaurant Co., and Hardy decided to retire. Without him though, its clientele fell away. So much so that in 1900 the owners very wisely persuaded him out of retirement to run their investment. This he did with his former success. Hardy died in 1921, and his widow continued to run the establishment with equal success for another five years. The Waterloo Bar finally closed its doors on 20 March 1926. On its final day, in a crowded house, the occasion marked by a number of presentations to Mrs Hardy, many spoke kindly words about her husband too. The proceedings terminated with the singing of *Auld Lang Syne*.

Joe Hillman's Stores, formerly known as the Town Hall Stores, was at the junction of New Street and Pinfold Street. It was a licensed victuallers of high standing in late nineteenth-century

Bragg's Wine Vaults, in the cellars of the Theatre Royal.

The Shakespeare, New Street, c. 1815.

Birmingham. Hillman had formerly worked at the Acorn Hotel, where he became known as the 'Demon Waiter' on account of his ability to carry more on a tray, at a greater speed, than any other waiter in the town. He could hold five glasses of ale in one hand. Hillman entered the Stores on 1 May 1862. Though rough and ready, with sawdust on the floor, Hillman's Stores was business-like and scrupulously clean. *Birmingham Faces & Places* describe the premises in almost affectionate detail:

> The low swinging doors, the entrance ankle deep in straw on muddy days, the counter, half of deal boards covered with oilcloth, the other half composed of barrels on end, the trestles worn well-nigh through with resting feet, and the tops shining with the elbows of whole generations of customers; the floor thick with fresh sawdust; the rooms opening one out of another in seemingly endless line, all roughly furnished with deal tables and kitchen chairs; the dingy roof, innocent of lath and plaster, and showing the bare joists; the cosy fire-places in unexpected corners; the bare black gas fittings with naked lights.

The Birmingham Musical Society and the Apollo Glee Union met at Hillman's for over twenty years.

In its long life no complaint was ever made against Hillman's to the authorities. No drunken man ever stayed there longer than the time occupied in showing him the door, and above all, no woman was ever served at the bar. The Stores was regrettably forced to close in 1888 for the building of the General Post Office. Joe Hillman later went on to keep the George Hotel in Solihull until well into the twentieth century.

The Royal Mail, at 84 New Street, took its name from the nearby General Post Office. An M&B house, it opened in December 1967. The pub, built into the shell of a former shop, has a second entrance at the rear in Pinfold Street. During May 2004, the Royal Mail received a long overdue refurbishment and change in name to the Isis. Just over a year later it was renamed the Bash Bar Lounge. The Shakespeare Tavern, established in the eighteenth century, faced the present Bennett's Hill. It became a popular meeting place, not only for drinking, but also for displays of bizarre forms of entertainment, including, in June 1788, a stone eater. He also ate tobacco pipes! In 1813 Madame Tussaud and her famous waxwork show stayed here. The house was rebuilt post-1818 and incorporated into the Theatre Royal. Bragg's Wine Vaults, which succeeded it, displayed the old Shakespeare Tavern sign above its entrance.

Bragg's Wine Vaults, in the cellars of the Theatre Royal in New Street, were not in the strictest sense of the word a public house. It was a wine bar, which in association with the Pit Bar in Lower Temple Street and the Circle and Gallery Bars, formed one of the Theatre Royal Bars. In addition to a fairly extensive cellar, the house also sold scotch and Irish whiskey, brandy, liqueurs and gin. It had a regular and respectable theatre-going clientele. The vaults were approached down a narrow staircase from the side of the theatre in New Street. The bar itself was long and narrow, upturned barrels acted as tables, with wooden crates acting as seats. It was curiously uncomfortable, but popular in its eccentricity. Bragg was a button maker by trade, who one day saw an advertisement in *The Times* by the captain of a merchant vessel. He had returned from the West Indies with a number of cases of excellent wine which he wished to sell or exchange for other commodities. Bragg offered a cargo of buttons, which was accepted, and the wine thus obtained was the stock in trade of his vaults. Bragg's closed in February 1904 for the extensive modernisation of the theatre.

The Grapes Tavern, a beerhouse, was next to the old grammar school in New Street. A lithograph of 1859, published by C. Graf of London, shows this two-storied Georgian house. There are no trade directory entries for this house.

The Grapes
Tavern, New
Street, 1852.

Above: *The Tavern in the Town, re-opened as Teddy's.*

Opposite: *The Lowenbrau Bier Keller – its opening night advertisement.*

The Tavern in the Town opened in November 1968. Councillor Dick Lawn was its first licensee. The entrance to the house is down a flight of steps to a large lounge area, which had formerly been the basement of Littlewood's department store. In November 1974 the Tavern and the nearby Mulberry Bush were bombed by the Provisional IRA. Twenty-one people were killed in the bombings. The Tavern was rebuilt and re-opened just over a year later as Teddy's. In 1978, following a £10,000 facelift, the pub changed its name to the Yard of Ale.

The last of the New Street public houses was the Fountain Inn, near the junction of High Street. In a sketch of c. 1870, the house is depicted as a two-storey Georgian premises with a large plain window to the ground floor and an entrance doorway to the right. In the mid-eighteenth century a Mr Swift kept the Fountain. During the Priestley Riot of 1791, William Hutton attempted to placate the mob by buying them beer from the Fountain. The beer was drunk, and the mob went on to burn John Baskerville's house at Easy Row. The Fountain became the Fountain Hotel under licensee William Whitaker in 1860, and was further renamed the Fountain Luncheon Stores under its last licensee James Gender. It closed in 1870. There were two beerhouses, their full address now unknown, the Horse & Groom, whose landlord Richard Dugmore died in November 1811, and the Crispin, the death of whose licensee, 'Mrs Phillips of the Sign of the Crispin, New Street', was recorded in the *Gazette* on 8 March 1793.

The new
Löwenbräu
Bier Keller
OPENS IN
BIRMINGHAM
ON
MARCH 24th, at 7p.m.
in NEEDLESS ALLEY OFF NEW ST.

BIRMINGHAM'S FIRST AUTHENTIC BIER KELLER
Live music, singing, entertainment,
traditional costumes, German wines
and spirits and superb
DRAUGHT LÖWENBRÄU BEER

Telephone   021-643 6751

The Wellington, Bennetts Hill.

Bennetts.

The Hill.

The Briar Rose.

Cannon Street, Needless Alley and Bennett's Hill

Just off New Street is Cannon Street, cut to provide access from New Street to the Baptist church, sited just below Temple Row. The Lamp Tavern must have been the earliest pub built along this little road. It dated from 1785, when William Shuter was listed as a licensed victualler at 39 Cannon Street, the Lamp's address. In 1849 the name of the house was changed to the Lamp Inn & Birmingham Cider Cellars. Henry Fulford's Gosta Green brewery took over the Lamp in 1884 and plans were drawn up to modernise it, subject to a renewal of lease. This did not happen, and the Lamp closed. In the rebuilding the Lamp was replaced by the Windsor. This was a delightful pub. Access was also from Needless Alley. The house opened in 1885 under licensee James Apsley Kingham. Architect William Wykes undertook alterations to the Windsor in April 1888. At lunchtime in the 1960s and '70s, the upstairs bar served as a dining room. In the evening it was used by its younger clientele. Originally an Atkinson's house, it was acquired by M&B when they took over the brewery in 1959. In the early 1990s PCPT Architects were brought in to 'redesign' the Windsor. Their solution was to simply gut the pub, two floors becoming one, all internal partitions torn out. Today it is huge, but soul-less. Wykes, who had undertaken work on the Lamp, was also brought in to do work on the Cannon, a little beerhouse, likewise cleared in 1885.

Much later replacements were the Parisian and Cagney's. The Parisian opened on 22 May 1970. An M&B house, it was built in the old machine room of the former Post & Mail building at a cost of £75,00. It was sited in a huge cellar, measuring 50ft x 30ft and 16ft high. Cagney's, a former office conversion for Davenport's, opened nearby in the 1980s. Very much of their time, and fleeting it was too, both the Parisian and Cagney's have now gone.

There is only one alley in Birmingham, and that is Needless. The exotically named Sultan's Divan, originally known as the Sultan's Stores, came into being in 1863 with George Humphris as its first licensee. Italian Joseph Cavorgna took over in 1865. Under him the house developed a somewhat sordid reputation. The Magistrates closed this bawdy-house down in 1874. The Lowenbrau Bier Keller, with genuine Munich-brewed Lowenbrau served in stoneware steins, opened in the Alley on 24 March 1970. It featured live entertainment with 'oomph bands', and staff in traditional Black Forest costumes. When leases fell due the bier keller moved on.

There were two little beerhouses in nineteenth-century Needless Alley, the Rose & Crown, in existence by 1870 under John Lyshon, and the Coal Hole. This house was situated halfway up the alley on the right-hand side as you walk up to Temple Row. It was there by 1870, according to the Rating Maps, but of course being a beerhouse is not named in the directories, which only list full public houses.

Bennetts Hill, cut c. 1800, was traditionally part of the commercial section of the town. All of its public houses are quite modern. The earliest was the Wellington, at 37 Bennetts Hill. Situated on the corner of Wellington Passage, it was opened in 1979 by London brewers Courage. The pub is named after the Duke of Wellington. The house was a conversion from a former bank. Situated in one large room, the area near the front window was raised on a dais, a couple of feet or so. In the 1990s the pub went into freefall when the brewers failed to spend the money necessary for its upkeep. It was rescued as a trendy wine bar called Kempson's, but such is the fickleness of the wine bar set, that when new wine bars opened, they moved on to new plains of shallowness, and Kempson's closed. But joy of joys, in the week before Christmas 2004, the premises re-opened as a free house, its old name restored. The bar is now on the right as you enter from Bennett's Hill, rather than on the left as previously. The choice of beers is phenomenal. The Factotem & Firkin was opened by the Firkin Brewery in the former Halifax

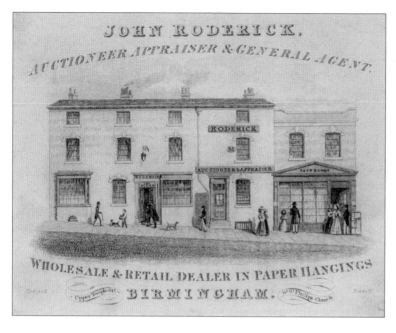

Left: *The Acorn Inn, Temple Street, 1825.*

Below left: *An advertisement for the Acorn Inn, c. 1890.*

Below right: *Murder at the Bodega, Temple Street*

ACORN

ALE, PORTER & LUNCHEON STORES

AND

DINING & NEWS ROOMS,

(ADJOINING THE HOTEL,)

UPPER TEMPLE STREET

AND

NEEDLESS ALLEY, BIRMINGHAM,

Within two minutes' walk of either Railway Station, the Theatre, Post Office, Town Hall, Bankruptcy and County Courts, and in the centre of the various Public Offices and Institutions of the town.

AN ORDINARY DAILY

AT HALF-PAST ONE O'CLOCK.

CHOP OR STEAK

AT FIVE MINUTES' NOTICE.

SOUPS FROM ELEVEN TILL ONE.

FIRST-CLASS BILLIARDS

RICHARD COLEMAN, Proprietor.

Gazette Dec. 6 —

HORRIBLE TRAGEDY IN A BIRMINGHAM LIQUOR VAULTS.

THE MANAGER SHOT DEAD BY A DISCHARGED BARMAN.

A tragedy which caused considerable consternation in Birmingham and district was enacted at the Bodega Vaults in Temple Street yesterday. Shortly after noon Police-sergeant Owen (A9), who was on duty in Temple Street, heard a report of firearms, and fearing some foul deed was being done, hastened in the direction from which the sound proceeded. As he ran towards the Bodega he heard a second report, and entering the vaults, saw several persons wresting from the possession of a young man named Herbert Edward Allen a revolver, which was still reeking with smoke, and lying near was the well-known form of the popular manager of the house, Mr. Henry James Skinner. The head barman, David Andrews, had just snatched the revolver from the grasp of Allen, who was in a most excited state, and as the officer appeared Andrews gave Allen into his custody, remarking, excitedly, "He has shot Mr. Skinner." The officer immediately despatched a messenger for a doctor, and a minute or so later Dr. Heaton, of Temple Row, was in attendance, but he could do no more than pronounce the victim of the outrage beyond the reach of medical assistance. During the interval which elapsed before the arrival of the doctor several of the persons present, many of whom were personal friends of Mr. Skinner, cut open his clothing when it was seen there was a bullet wound on the right side of the body and one on the left, the latter having apparently penetrated the heart. On hearing the doctor's declaration that Mr. Skinner was dead, the police sent for an ambulance, and on it the body was conveyed to the Moor Street mortuary, and the young barman Allen was conveyed to the lock-up at Newton Street.

THE MANNER OF THE MURDER.

The deputy-manager of the vaults, Mr. David Andrews, explained to a reporter later in the day that on Tuesday last Mr. Skinner told Allen, who is 25 years of age, and lived at 17, Upper Gough Street, and his brother, Arthur John Allen, also employed at the establishment as a barman, that in consequence of their conduct they must leave at once, and they were told to come on Wednesday for the wages due to them. They called upon Mr. Skinner as directed, and Arthur received the money due to him, but Herbert, generally known amongst the Bodega customers as Bert, was told to come again on the following day, as he was then under the influence of drink, and very excited. When the premises were opened yesterday morning the brothers were waiting outside, and Mr. Skinner then paid Herbert what was due to him. Apparently Herbert then started on a drinking bout, and shortly before 12 o'clock Arthur visited the Victoria Courts, and took out a summons against Mr. Skinner for an assault alleged to have been committed on Tuesday night before they left. This summons was taken out only a few minutes or so before noon, and a few minutes later the brothers were seen together in Temple Street, near the Bodega. Mr. Skinner was outside as Herbert came up, and the two entered into conversation which a bystander states was very heated on the part of the young fellow who now stands accused of murdering his late employer. Mr. Skinner went inside the vaults, and Herbert Allen followed him and requested to be supplied with a drink. Mr. Skinner was appealed to by the under manager as to whether he should be served, and he gave it as his opinion that Allen had already had sufficient, and must have no more. This appears to have angered the young man considerably, for he called, "Here, Mr. Skinner!" Mr. Skinner, with a motion of his right hand, put him off, evidently wishing to have nothing more to say to him.

THE VICTIM.

MR. H. J. SKINNER.

THE MURDERER.

HERBERT EDWARD ALLEN.

Building Society offices in April 1997. It was their 150th pub. The pub was aimed at the lunchtime trade of local business people. A bitter called Factotem (ABV 4.3%) was specially brewed for the house. With the Firkin split, the house was renamed the Hill. Bennett's, on the corner of Bennett's Hill and Waterloo Street, was formerly the National Westminster Bank, and before that the National Provincial Bank. The building is Grade II★ listed. Designed in 1833 by C.R. Cockrell, it was rebuilt in 1869 and 1890 to the designs of John Gibson. The interior is a 1920s neo-Grecian/Egyptian style. Its entrance is particularly splendid, with Corinthian pilasters, frieze panels in its arched entrance and a sculptured ceiling. Bought by Marston's Brewery, it was converted into a pub at a cost of £1 million, and opened as Bennett's in August 1997. The Briar Rose is a Weatherspoon's house, opened in December 1999, at a cost of £1 million. Its name is taken from a series of paintings and a stained-glass window by Sir Edward Burne Jones who was born in 1833, just across the road from the pub. The Briar Rose was formerly the Abbey National Bank which closed in 1996.

Temple Row and Street

Temple Street derived its name from a pagoda-like structure in the Cherry Orchard near St Philip's Cathedral. The Old Royal Hotel was at 26 Temple Row. The Hotel, as it was originally known, was erected in 1772 by a Tontine subscription, whereby the last remaining member of the financing group gained the hotel. The first tenants were Messrs Dadley & Palmer, who carried on the business until 1790. William Styles succeeded them. It was a dinner here on 4 July 1791 that sparked off the Priestley Riots. The hotel windows were smashed by the rioters, who went on to set fire to the homes of a number of prominent Nonconformists, in the belief that they supported the French Revolution. In 1802, Admiral Lord Nelson stayed here with Sir William and Lady Hamilton. The hotel became the Royal Hotel in 1805, following the visit of HRH the Duke of Gloucester. Other visitors included the Grand Duchess of Oldenburgh, sister of Tsar Alexander, in 1814, and the Duchess of Kent and Princess Victoria (later Queen Victoria) in 1830. During its time the hotel was known by a number of names, including Styles Royal Hotel and Dee's Hotel. The Royal Hotel closed in December 1959 and was demolished in 1964. The name was transferred by M&B to the Red Lion in Church Street.

At the other end of Temple Row, at its junction with Bull Street, was the White Swan. It was a mid-eighteenth-century tavern, with its main entrance in Temple Row. In its day it was noted for its 'Tenpenny Ale' and its good-natured, long-term licensee, Thomas Jones. After Jones retired, the house was taken by Edward Cope, a wine and spirit merchant, formerly licensee of premises in the High Street. The tavern trade was relinquished, and the house became a gin shop.

Returning back around the crescent to its junction with Temple Street, was the Clarendon Vaults, at 7 Temple Row. This public house was in existence by 1819, but known then as the Globe. The change of name took place post-1830. By 1863 Vaults had been dropped in favour of the more prestigious name of Hotel. So it was to be for the next 100 years until the lapse of the lease in 1963, and the hotel's closure and demolition.

The Acorn at 32 Temple Street dated from 1750. Its first known owner was a Mrs Rawley, a widow, who with her death in 1766 was succeeded by Charles Friend. John Roderick, an auctioneer, bought the house in 1824. He purchased the premises next door too, and the Acorn Inn became the Acorn Hotel. Roderick kept the house until 1832, when his brother-in-law, Thomas Chambers, a former draper in Bull Street, took over. Later licensees include William Evans, a former footman to Birmingham's first MP, Thomas Atwood. Thomas Prideaux followed him as licensee in 1851. He opened the Acorn Vaults in the rear of the hotel, facing onto Needless Alley. These same Vaults were updated from the drawings of architect William Hale from plans prepared by him on 8 August 1878. James Clements, another auctioneer, took over the hotel from Prideaux, expanding into 33 and 33½ Temple Street. Local historian Eliezer Edwards, in his *Old Taverns of Birmingham*, wrote of the Acorn:

> Before the floor was lowered, the height of the smoking room was only seven or eight feet. It was lighted at night by candles, one of which, with its necessary accompaniment, a pair of snuffers, stood on each table. The candlesticks in which they were placed were nearly two feet high. When the tall candles which were used were first lighted the flames reached to within a short distance of the ceiling. When there were a dozen or twenty smokers at work the atmosphere of the low room was so dense that it was not easy to distinguish the features of those who sat far away. In Mr Roderick's time he always sat in the centre chair at the top of the room, the table which stood there being distinguished by having two candles. At eight o'clock of every evening, except Saturday and Sunday, silence was called, and he proceeded to read aloud the most interesting items of the London evening papers of the previous day. Saturday was excepted because on that evening there was what was then called a free-and-easy.

The old hotel was demolished and a new house was built to the design of Smethwick architects Wood & Kendrick. In 1909 the name of the hotel was changed to the Imperial Hotel. As a token of affection for the earlier establishment, the hotel bar was named the Acorn. The Imperial has now been demolished, and replaced by clothes shops.

One modern, one old; the Lamp Tavern was in existence in Temple Street in 1767 with Thomas Moore as licensee, Red, formerly the Plantation, formerly the Sputnik, is a somewhat nondescript public house at the top of Temple Street. The Bodega was established in 1882, taking over the old premises of T&E Spittle's Dining Rooms. The Bodega is best remembered for a bloody murder that occurred here on 5 December 1895. A young barman, Herbert Edward Allen, recently dismissed for bad conduct, returned a few days later for his wages. He had been drinking, and manager Henry James Skinner refused to serve him. Allen pulled a gun and shot Skinner dead. The murderer escaped the death penalty on the grounds of insanity. In 1897 the premises were sold to Trocadero Ltd, and the establishment was renamed the Trocadero. The original building had been constructed as part of a four-storey Italianate palazzo in 1854 by Samuel Hemmings for the Unity Insurance Co. About 1902 the present ground-floor front of glazed yellow tiles, mosaic and stained glass in the Art Nouveau style, was added, supposedly by Maw & Co. During the post-Second World War period, and into the 1970s, the Troc had a certain Gay evening atmosphere, at a time when such practices were still illegal in this country. The fraternity have now moved out to Hurst Street, leaving the Troc to its quiet respectability.

Crossing New Street and down into Lower Temple Street, is the Shakespeare. The original pub was a narrow-fronted three-storey Georgian house, with a slight single bow window, its entrance door to the right. Above the doorway entrance was a large lantern. This is the view portrayed in a pen and wash drawing by Birmingham artist A. Tarlington in 1870. The Shakespeare was taken over by M&B who, acquiring the premises next door, demolished the two structures and built the late Victorian pub that we see today. The house acquired a full license in 1915.

Immediately next door to the Shakespeare was the Temple Bar. A former beer and wine-licensed premises until 1951, when landlady Helen Burleigh purchased a full license at a cost of £2,500. Originally the Temple Bar was an Atkinson's house, opened in 1928, but was taken over by M&B in 1959. It had a small, low-roofed front bar, with an upstairs dining room. In the evening the upstairs room was used by its younger customers. The Temple Bar was noted for the quality of its Guinness, and its slightly diffuse clientele. It closed in 2001 and was converted into a shoe shop.

The Trocadero, Temple Street, formerly the Bodega.

The Shakespeare, Lower Temple Street.

The Old Joint Stock, Temple Row.

The Fountain was at 21 Lower Temple Street. Licensee William Mortimer first appears as such in the trade directory of 1812, where he is listed as a 'dealer in bottled cyder and perry'. He was succeeded by Samuel Shaw, and upon his death his widow Elizabeth ran the house until 1830. She sold up to Henry Welling, who sold to Samuel Clark in 1834. Clark appears to have been the last licensee.

The Garrick's Head was at No. 27, and was named after the eighteenth century actor-manager David Garrick (1717-79). It was very close to the site of the present day Shakespeare. James Sly was landlord from 1785 until 1791. The Garrick closed in 1873.

Situated on the left-hand corner of Lower Temple Street and Stephenson Street was the Green Man. It was an early eighteenth-century building of two and a half storeys, with attic windows in the roof. In its later life it had prominent large multi-paned glass windows. The words 'Green Man Tavern' was painted on the wall at first-floor level. There is an obituary for one-time licensee, James Clarke, who died in October 1821.

Returning back up Temple Street and left into Temple Row, before we reach Colmore Row we come to the Old Joint Stock at 4 Temple Row. A Fuller's house, it was originally built in 1862-3 to a design by Birmingham architect J.A. Chatwin for the Birmingham Joint Stock Bank. The bank was taken over by Lloyd's Bank, but relinquished by them in the 1990s, being surplus to requirements. The building was bought by London brewers Fuller's of Chiswick, and was successfully converted into a pub. Architecturally it makes full use of the original palatial banking hall, with an added mezzanine space to the rear. The long central bar is very much a London feature. In addition to Fuller's ales, the Joint Stock also sells the beers of former Birmingham brewers, Beowulf.

Colmore Row

Colmore Row has known many names. In the eighteenth century the end nearest Snow Hill was known as Bull Lane. It was later renamed Monmouth Street. The end nearest New Street was called New Hall Lane and Bewdley Street. That part between St Philip's and Newhall Street was Ann Street. Near the site of the present Council House it was called both Mount Pleasant and the Hay Market. It is only from the 1880s that the street as a whole became Colmore Row. Back in 1767, as Sketchley's Birmingham Directory reveals, the Great Coat was at Mount Pleasant. Job Phillips was its landlord. In the directory of 1770 the address of this house is given as 34 Mount Pleasant. Also in 1767 was Henry Timmins' Horse & Jockey in Bull Lane, and George Cracknal's Blue Bell at 5 Colmore Row. Cracknal was there until 1777, when he sold the pub to Robert Moore.

The Bricklayer's Arms was at 13 Ann Street. It dated from c. 1769, when John Reeves was listed as a publican here. By 1777 he had handed over to his son, Thomas. In August 1800 the house was sold at auction by Thomas Warren. George Clews was landlord from 1827 to 1830. Henry Oxford followed him as landlord, and he was followed by Thomas Tabberner. By 1860, under Henry Lawrence, the name of the house was changed to the Old Bricklayer's Arms, to distinguish it from two other pubs of the same name in the immediate vicinity. By the 1860s most of the leases on the properties along this road fell due. The Bricklayer's Arms closed in 1867.

The Bell & Candlesticks was at 35 Ann Street. It was a two-and-a-half-storey house, opened in 1817. William Westwood was its first landlord. In 1843 a house called The Stores is listed as being

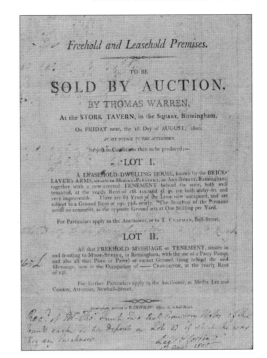

Right: *Auction of the Bricklayers Arms, Ann Street.*

Below: *The Town Hall Tavern, Ann Street, to the right of Bryan's shop.*

THE CORNER OF ANN STREET & CONGREVE STREET · 1855

at this address. That same directory, Slater's, also lists a pub called the Coal Hole as being here too. These appear to be erroneous entries. The lease of the Bell & Candlesticks expired in 1872. Charles Godfrey, there for over thirty years, was its last licensee.

The White Lion at 41 Ann Street dated from post-1823, with Mary Wilson as landlady. The house was sold off in 1834 and re-opened in 1835 as the Town Hall Tavern, under William Webster. The name was taken from the nearby Town Hall, opened that same year. Charles Cork was landlord during the early 1840s. Mrs Ann Whiles, and daughter Elizabeth, had taken over by 1848. They ran the house over the next fifteen years, being replaced as licensee by Mrs Annie Whitehouse in 1862. She was here until the closure of the Town Hall Tavern in 1873 for the building of the Council House.

There were a further two beerhouses in Ann Street; The Woodman and the Free Church Tavern. The Woodman has come to light because of the obituary notice of Sophia, the forty-eight-year-old wife of licensee Henry Vaughan, who died on 13 December 1847. The Free Church Tavern was named after the newly opened Christchurch, situated on the corner of Colmore Row and New Street. Unlike most other Church of England churches, there was no charge for pews. James Gutteridge was landlord in 1818. Also in Colmore Row was the Bell Inn, seemingly a beerhouse, and not listed in the trade directories. There is an obituary, on 27 April 1807, relating to its former landlady, 'Mrs Manders'. The White Hart was at 18 Colmore Row, just facing St Philip's church. It dated from c. 1808. John Hartley was licensee then, up to 1812. He was succeeded by George Webb, who in turn was followed by his son when he retired. His widow, Mary, continued to run the pub until its closure in 1842. St Philip's Tavern appears to have been very close to the White Hart. It opened post-1812; Joseph Bower, who died in late October 1819, is its only known licensee. The Grand Hotel, which closed in 2005, always had a public bar. Its entrance (the bar is still open), is in Barwick Street. The Great Western Hotel, which fronted Snow Hill Station, also had a public bar, which was established in 1880 with John Williams as licensee.

The Great Western Vaults at 9 Monmouth Street began life as the Dolphin. Isaac Morris was landlord from 1786 until his death in September 1793. Its last landlord, and first, as the Great Western Vaults, was John Currier. The change of name took place in 1853. As the twentieth century approached, the name of the house was shortened to the Great Western. The house closed in 1911 as part of Neville Chamberlain's 'fewer but better' scheme. Henry Stephens was the Great Western's final licensee. As a replacement for all these lost pubs, it was not until the 1960s and the completion of the Inner Ring Road that a new public house was built. It was the Brown Derby, a theme pub, reflecting the theatrical world of the 1920s. The pub was reached by a pedestrian subway in Colmore Circus. From the exterior it was a rather forbidding black marble block with a red door. The bar had a low oppressive ceiling, the juke box was always on, the beer was keg. So, there is nothing really nice to say about the place. The Brown Derby closed, and was demolished when Colmore Circus was again redeveloped at the start of the twenty-first century.

The Colmore Estate within the Ring Road

Manzoni's perfidious Inner Ring Road cut right through the Colmore Estate, using Great Charles Street as its northern boundary. It is hoped that pubs beyond Great Charles Street will be dealt with in a future book.

Little Charles Street, came into being in the late eighteenth century and became an extension of Edmund Street post-1870. There are three known eighteenth-century pubs in this street. The

Bushwackers, Edmund Street.

The former White Swan, Edmund Street.

The Old Contemptibles, Edmund Street.

Fire Engine, situated near the corner of Livery Street, is listed in the directories from 1767 to 1777, with John Beardmore as licensee. The Dublin Tavern dated from *c.* 1770, its last known licensee was James Curnin in 1818. The Golden Cup was a 1772 house, whose first landlord, Robert Willis, died in February 1781. His successor as landlord was John Proctor. As the century progressed, Little Charles Street had a somewhat racy reputation, being what is now known as a 'red-light' district. So it was very much welcomed by the Authorities when leases along this road began falling due from the late 1860s. The Golden Cup closed in 1870, as likewise did the Royal Oak at 62 Little Charles Street. It was in existence by 1817. Abraham Knowles was its landlord then. The house is noted for being the one-time 1830s home of millionaire pen maker Joseph Gillott. The Plumbers Arms was at No. 23. It was a beerhouse, dating from 1855, under James Ovens. It was demolished in 1870, but the license was retained, and a new house was built on the site. The license was finally surrendered in 1892 under a further Improvement Scheme. The Horse & Groom was a beerhouse, in existence in 1824 with John Griffiths as its landlord. At 40 Little Charles Street was the Horse & Jockey, dating from *c.* 1828 under licensee David Stokes. Like the others, the Horse & Groom was closed down when its lease fell due in 1870. At 57 Little Charles Street was the Malt Shovel. Joseph Green was landlord, 1848-1851. In the slightly re-aligned and redeveloped Edmund Street, which now stretched from Easy Row to Livery Street, were some twenty or so public houses. Starting on the south-western side of the road, up near the Town Hall at what in 1878 was then 40 Edmund Street, was the Wein Keller. As its name suggests, it was a wine bar that also sold spirits. It was established by Richard Horley in 1878. His widow, Basilia Horley, took over in 1882, but by 1885 the fizz had gone out of the venture.

The Corner House, formerly the Hogs Head, Edmund Street.

Carpe Diem, Great Charles Street.

The Hope & Anchor was opened in 1762 when that part of Edmund Street up by the Town Hall was known as Harlow Street. The original Georgian house was of two storeys, with a large bow window, and entrance doorway to the right. There was only one window on the floor above, with a projecting chevron sign occupying the site where one might rightly suppose another window to be. When Ansells took over the house they completely remodelled the front, yet left the pub itself intact. Alterations to the front were carried out to designs of architect C.J. Hodson from his plans of 21 August 1893. In its oak-panelled 'Gentlemen Only' bar, aldermen and councillors met to unofficially discuss the business of city. The Hope & Anchor was once run by a former alderman, Eli Fletcher, who held the license for more than thirty-four years; so long in fact that the house was alternatively known as Eli's. The Fletcher family had run the pub for over one hundred years. The Hope & Anchor closed its doors for the last time on 27 June 1965. It was demolished for the building of the present Central Library. The Wilsons, the last licensees, moved to the Wellington in Bristol Street.

The Rodney, at 84 Edmund Street, opened in 1820. Its owner John Payton was originally a wood turner. The pub was situated in that part of Edmund Street up by the present Council House and Central Library. When William Eaves was licensee in 1867 the site was compulsory purchased, and the house closed. Situated between Congreve Street and Church Street were the Odd Fellows' Arms and the Dog & Duck. The Odd Fellows' Arms was at 54 Edmund Street, and was in existence in 1848 under licensee Tom Brown. The Dog & Duck, at 55, was in existence as early as 1767 under licensee Thomas Darcy. Over the next one hundred years until its closure in 1866, it had a further ten licensees. On the corner of Newhall Street is Pals; more of which later under Newhall Street. Crossing over Newhall Street to the old 1896 red-

The Litten Tree, Newhall Street.

All Bar One, Newhall Street.

brick and terracotta National Telephone Company's offices, designed by Martin & Chamberlain, we arrive at Bushwackers, which opened in January 2003. This bar and restaurant is part of a chain of such establishments based in Worcester. As the name suggests, it has an Australian theme. Crossing over Barwick Street was the old White Swan. Now closed, and largely demolished, the façade still remains, the swan motif still visible above its central column. It originated in around 1811 under licensee John Griffis, and closed with George Bulpitt, the third generation of the same family who had been landlords here. The old road was cleared, and re-aligned as an extension of Edmund Street. A new White Swan was built for Atkinson's, and William Proctor was put in as landlord. A smoke room was added in March 1890 from designs submitted by J.S. Davis. The White Swan became an M&B house in 1959. The company sub-leased the premises to Berni Inns in 1968. During the 1970s the cellar was converted into a not very convincing bier keller. While others offered Loewenbrau, The White Swan offered Brew XI. The license of the White Swan was surrendered on 24 March 1999, and the house has now been redeveloped as offices.

On the other side of the street on the corner with Livery Street is the Old Contemptibles, at 176 Edmund Street. The first house on the site was the Adelphi (Wine) Vaults, which despite its name was a late eighteenth-century beerhouse. It closed when the corner was redeveloped. The Albion Hotel was built on the same site in the new development. The new house was designed by William Hale in 1880, and was later taken over by M&B. The change in name to the Old Contemptibles took place on 31 January 1953. It was a derisory name given by the German Kaiser to the British Expeditionary Force, following the Battle of Mons. The soldiers for their part accepted the name as an honourable title. The Birmingham survivors of the BEF regularly held their meetings there after the change in name, until, in an act of meanness, Bass decided that they did not want these old men there any longer. Since then the place has gone downhill (as if cursed), with an almost constant change of managers. As at Christmas 2005, the house was up for sale. In its day the Old Cons was an exceptional pub, with a rather splendid long bar, and paintings on the walls. Ideally it needs a new owner who is sympathetic to what is there, and update it accordingly.

Back up to the corner of Newhall Street is the Corner House, formerly the Hogs Head. It was the ground-floor conversion of the old Scottish Mutual Assurance Co., designed by F.B. Osborn in 1895. A four-storey late Victorian building with iron railings on its upper storeys, above the doorway is a tower surmounted by a cupola. Inside it follows the Hogs Head formula of scrubbed pine and an odd miscellany of tables and chairs. Saturday lunchtime is a good time to have a quiet pint or two and read the daily newspapers. On the other corner of Newhall Street was the Waggon & Horses, at what was then 23 Edmund Street. Thomas Freeman was licensee from 1812 to 1830. The lease appears to have expired in 1866, and the house was closed. At 24 Edmund Street was the London Tavern, a beerhouse, there in 1870 with William Proverbs as landlord. The Lamp Tavern of 1818 was situated somewhere nearby. Charles Griffiths was its landlord. The Watchmakers Arms, a beerhouse, was in this part of Edmund Street in 1870.

Of some curiosity was the Druid's Head, near the junction with Margaret Street. It is believed to have been built between 1760-70. At this beerhouse the Druids' Lodge No. 17 met, under landlord John Barber. It was he who added the semi-circular building at the rear. The Druid's Head was demolished for the building of the Museum & Art Gallery.

The Lamb was situated three doors down from the Druid's Head, and was also demolished for the building of the museum. Of particular note, the Lamb was the home of the Artisans' Library, a working men's library of educational and morally uplifting works. The last of the known pubs and beerhouses in Edmund Street was the Crown at 78 Edmund Street. Situated near the Town Hall, William Ward was licensee in 1818. The house survived until 1869, when with its lease falling due, it was closed and later demolished.

The Queen's Arms,
Newhall Street.

Cornwall Street runs parallel to Edmund Street. There is one contemporary public house here, the Metro Bar at 73 Cornwall Street. It is a very good conversion of an elegant four-storey Victorian building, tucked away just behind the Museum & Art Gallery. The lower end of Cornwall Street, bordering onto Livery Street, was originally known as Bread Street. The Rose & Crown was here at No. 43. Established by 1828, John Newton was its licensee. In 1878-79, new owner Thomas Fisher had built a new and improved public house to the designs of Mallins, a Birmingham firm of architects. A few brief years later though the area was cleared in an Improvement Scheme. Lying in between Cornwall Street and Great Charles Street is Market Street. There was a pub here, the Coach & Horses, from *c.* 1765. It was not until 1835 that, though numbered, the house was also named. Sarah Chirm was its landlady.

Great Charles Street is the spinal road of the Colmore Estate. The Inner Ring Road cut through and widened it, and left some ugly scars. Only one public house has been opened here, and that some thirty years or so after the cutting of the road. The Carpe Diem (the name is Latin for 'seize the day'), is situated on the corner of Market Street. It opened in the ground

The Red Lion, Church Street, 1886.

floor of a renovated office block. The décor has lots of empty wine bottles, but this should not deter the determined beer drinker; there is usually some interesting cask beer. Of the houses lost there are at least six. St Philip's Tavern, 35 Great Charles Street on the corner with Church Street, opened in 1834, with John Midlam as landlord. It closed when the lease fell due in 1877. The Old Crown was on the other side of the street at its junction with Ludgate Hill. It was in existence by 1818. Changes were made to the house in 1883 from plans drawn up by architect J. Allen. The license of the house was temporarily withdrawn in 1892 when Ludgate Hill was widened. The license restored, the house continued to pull pints until 1913. On the other corner with Ludgate Hill was the Chapel Tavern, taking its name from St Paul's chapel at the other end of the hill. It is first recorded in 1828, when Thomas Partridge was its licensee. The house was taken over by Butler's Crown Brewery of Broad Street in 1897, and later following the merger became an M&B house. Demolished under the Improvement Scheme described above, it was rebuilt as a three-storey house to the design of architect Thomas Sabat from his plans of July 1891. The Chapel Tavern closed its doors in July 1965 for the cutting of the Inner Ring Road. Right down Great Charles Street's hill, on the corner with Livery Street, was the Golden Lion. William Hanson was licensee in 1818. The Golden Lion closed with the expiry of it lease in 1872. At 115 Great Charles Street in 1817 was the Sampson & Lion, under William Parker. Built in a converted house, its lease fell due in 1867 and it was demolished. The Bricklayers Arms was in existence by 1791 under licensee George Moore. He had an obituary notice in the *Gazette*

The Old Royal, formerly the Red Lion, Church Street.

in November 1800. During his time as licensee, the house was used as the meeting place of the Nightly Patrol Association, who formed a security force to protect their property; this at a time when Birmingham had a population of 60,000 but only two constables. The Bricklayers closed in 1852, probably due to an expiration of lease.

Bisecting Great Charles Street is Newhall Street. As such the street is now divided by the Inner Ring Road. For convenience the street is treated as a complete entity. Turning the corner from Colmore Row into Newhall Street was the Litten Tree. Originally a 1970s nightclub called Pollyannas, it evolved into a pub, and eventually became a free house. It closed in November 2005 when the owners failed to renew their lease. Digress, formerly Pals, is situated on the corner with Edmund Street on the ground floor of a 1960s office block. Sofas are much in evidence. Digress is female-friendly, as you can see when you walk by. All Bar One, the last of the new generation of pubs, is situated on the corner with Cornwall Street. It is part of the M&B stable of pubs-cum-wine bars. A conversion from a former commercial building, it has large clear windows out onto both streets. Bass opened a second All Bar One in Brindley Place in November 1998.

Older pubs now. The Lord Byron, also known as the Byron's Head, was named after poet Lord George Byron (1788-1824). In existence by 1839, under Richard Poole, there is an obituary to his daughter, Ann, in the *Birmingham Gazette* of 8 June 1846. The Mitre was at 66 Newhall Street. There is a short death notice for one-time licensee 'Mrs Lunn' in the 15 March 1802 edition of the *Gazette*. She had succeeded her husband James, who died in 1800. John Gilbert, and later his wife, Harriett, ran the house for twenty-five years, from 1835 to 1859. The Mitre closed in 1869, its lease having terminated. The Falcon, which opened in 1853 with Joseph Underwood as licensee, was at 71 Newhall Street. The lease on this Colmore Estate house fell due in 1867, when Mrs Elizabeth Richards was landlady, and the Falcon was closed.

The Queen's Arms is situated on the corner of Charlotte Street. It was opened in 1820 on a one-hundred-year lease, issued by the Colmore Estate. The house was later taken over by M&B and completely rebuilt in 1901 to a design by architect Joseph Wood. Of special note to those who lived through the dark days of silly closing times, the Queen's Arms situated right next door to the old Science Museum was noted for its all-day opening when the Science Museum had a 'Steam Day'. A late Victorian pub, it has a splendid cartouche at first-floor level on the corner of the two streets, with 'Mitchells and Butlers Gold Medal Ales' written in relief. Inside it has retained much of its original Victoriana.

Church Street, running parallel to Newhall Street, takes its name from St Philip's church, now the Anglican Cathedral. Of the public houses here there was a veritable menagerie. The White Hart was established at 21 Church Street by 1869, under landlord Augustus Grew. There was the Tiger at 47 Church Street between 1818 and 1870. There was the White Swan at 1 Church Street. Edward Venables was licensee in 1807. This house was kept at one time by Edward Bingley, who was arrested for coining, by George Redfern, a well-known head constable in Birmingham during the early nineteenth century. Bingley and his two confederates were later hanged for their crime at Warwick. Redfern, it is said, later married Bingley's widow, and became an innkeeper. The house, situated on the corner of Great Charles Street, was rebuilt, but closed in 1892 for road widening. The Roebuck was here from 1767, when John Cart was listed as landlord. The house appears to have been renamed the Church Tavern, and was here until 1830. The Beehive Stores, a beerhouse, surrendered its license in 1892 under the Improvement Scheme, when Church Street was widened. The George & Dragon opened in 1820, with Henry Chambers as licensee. He remained here until his death in 1852, at the age of sixty-seven. His widow took over the license, remaining for a further nine years, thus making a total of forty-one years between them. The license was surrendered in 1892. The Red Lion at the junction of Church Street and Bread Street was built c. 1775. Its reputation began with the arrival of Mr Litchfield in 1780. He had formerly been landlord of the Three Crowns in Deritend. Under him the house gained an enviable reputation. For nearly one hundred years the Red Lion remained in the possession of the extended family. Litchfield relinquished control of the hotel to his son-in-law, John Barlow, a former metal roller in Hampton Street. Barlow was not much of a landlord, so the license was passed onto another son-in-law, Tom Birch. He was better suited to the task. Upon his death his widow, Litchfield's daughter, took up the reins. Upon her death her younger brother, Joseph Litchfield, took charge. He continued as landlord until 1877 when the old Red Lion passed out of family hands, and was taken over by Harriet Usborne.

The Red Lion is best known for being the spiritual home of the British Association for the Advancement of Science. This scientific and literary society was founded in 1831. It meets annually at one of the principal cities of the United Kingdom. In 1839 it met at Birmingham. There was a breakaway movement of some of the younger members under Edward Forbes, who objected to the expense and formality of the occasion, and adjourned to the less expensive Red Lion. Here they dined more cheaply, their meals enlivened by jokes and songs. A decade later the Association returned to Birmingham and made the Red Lion their headquarters once more. In 1883, as part of the Improvement Scheme for the town, the authorities decided that the house should be 'rebuilt to meet the requirements of a better class of business on the existing or such larger area as the Justices may approve'. The houses either side, in Church Street and Bread

Street, were demolished and the Red Lion was extended. Bread Street was later redeveloped and became an extension of Cornwall Street. The Red Lion closed in 1898. A couple of years later a second public house of the same name was built on the other side of Church Street, at its junction with Cornwall Street. The new house was designed by Arthur Hamblin, and built 1899-1900. It is a visual delight in red brick and cream terracotta, with gables and pediments, in a mock Jacobean style. There is much stained glass and above its corner entrance is a turret with a conical top, surmounted by a lion weather vane, reflecting its original name. A change in name occurred in 1964 when the Old Royal Hotel in Temple Row was demolished and M&B transferred the name to the Red Lion at 53 Church Street. Sympathetically refurbished during the 1990s, the Old Royal has an entry in the *Good Beer Guide* for 2006.

Of the remaining public houses in Church Street there was the Bell at No. 25, opened by Joseph Hatkinds in 1767. He was later followed by John Cart, late landlord of the Roe Buck. The Lamp had opened by 1785 when Francis Turner was entered as licensee. A beerhouse, it was still there in 1790, but either closed or had a change in name soon after. Nock's Hotel was built on a one-hundred-year lease issued by the Colmore Estate. It went in the 1870s redevelopment. The Colmore Rest, a beerhouse, was at an unspecified site in Church Street. It may eventually have become the Colmore Inn. Additions were carried out to the house in 1899, from drawings submitted by A.H. Hamblin. The Colmore Inn, as mentioned, was licensed in 1903 as the Colmore Hotel. It was an M&B house. It inherited a lot of comfortable old armchairs and tables when the Woodman in Easy Row closed, along with a lot of its customers, who enjoyed its old world charm. On 14 November 1969, now refurbished, the house re-opened as the Gaiety; its original Victoriana ripped out to be replaced by kitsch Victoriana. In 1990 it became the Cathedral Tavern following another makeover. In 1999 Bass, its then owners, sold the pub to Tarmac, along with their other nearby pub, the White Swan in Edmund Street, for office development. The Colmore's license was surrendered on 24 March 1999.

Livery Street

Livery Street formed the eastern boundary of the Colmore Estate. The road is named after Swann's Riding Academy and Livery, which opened pre-1787 and stood at the corner of what was to become Cornwall Street. There is an echo of the old livery in the pub known as the Horse & Groom. It is first recorded in 1818, with Thomas Holdback as its licensee. It survived up to 1855. Dating from 1800, the landlady of the Waggon & Horses in 1829, Mrs Ann Bacon, also let out horse and carriages. There were some early beerhouses here in Livery Street. The Rose appears in an advertisement in *Aris's Gazette* for 1791. The Bear & Grapes likewise appears in the newspaper for that year, when it acted as an exchange centre for 'all sorts of Birmingham, Walsall, Bloxwich, Wolverhampton, and Redditch goods for all sorts of hosiery and haberdashery.' The Freeman's Tavern appeared in the paper in the following year when an obituary notice was placed relating to the 'Widow Smith' of that same pub. She had been landlady from 1785. The Blue Bell makes a brief appearance in the Birmingham trade directory for 1818-20, with Richard Palmer as licensee. A later nineteenth-century pub, the Swan With Two Necks, was run by Alf Greenfield, a well-known professional boxer. Alf taught boxing in a makeshift ring out in the yard. He also had a rat pit out at the back, where terriers were matched to kill rats at four pence a rat. The Albion Wine Vaults opened in the mid-1850s. Henry Herridge was its first licensee. He remained there until 1886, licensee of the same premises for over thirty years. The name was

The Albion Vaults, Livery Street.

changed to the Albion Commercial Hotel following refurbishment, but by 1904 it had reverted to its original name. The last trade directory entry for the house was in 1908.

The Three Tuns opened under licensee Joseph Longman in 1818. Thomas George, whose short death notice appears in the *Gazette* in March 1824, followed him. His widow took over following his death, then there was George Penn, the Gays, John Holliday, and Peter Taylor. Samuel Scandret was the last landlord of the Three Tuns, which closed in 1872.

The Railway Tavern was on the corner of Mary Ann Street and Livery Street. Birmingham artist, Paul Braddon, shows a sketch of this house viewed from beneath the nearby railway arch. He depicts a three-storey pub, with a large window onto each street frontage, and a central door on the corner. Architect A.H. Hamblin, drew up plans for changes to the house on 27 October 1899.

On the corner with Great Charles Street was the White Horse at 203 Livery Street. It opened with John Jones as its licensee in 1828. The White Horse closed in 1850-51. The Jolly Sailor was on the corner with Henrietta Street. As well as selling beer, the house also acted as an occasional auction house. In an advertisement in *Aris's Gazette* for 16 January 1797 various household items, such as furniture and stoves, were offered for sale.

The Bell, at 101 Livery Street, was a Davenport's house, featured in their house magazine, *Malt & Hops*, in November 1947. There were photographs of landlord 'Mr Gair', his son Joseph, and 'Jim the jovial barman'. Richard Gair, landlord from 1941 to 1949, was an ex-soldier, having served his time on the North West Frontier. He was wounded and invalided back home. He got a job at Davenport's in 1930, and was eventually offered the license of the Bell. It was an early nineteenth-century public house, dating from around 1812. Alterations and additions were carried out to the Bell during 1880, from drawings prepared by architect William Jenkins, for licensee David Dagley. The house was later rebuilt for new owners Davenport's, to the designs of well-known pub architects James & Lister Lea, and reinstated with a full license in 1896. The Bell closed in 1964.

PETER S. TAYLOR,
LICENSED VICTUALLER,
"THREE TUNS" INN,
90, LIVERY STREET, BIRMINGHAM.
N.B.—BEDS AND REFRESHMENTS ON REASONABLE TERMS.

Advertisement for the Three Tuns, Livery Street.

The Bell, Livery Street, November 1947.

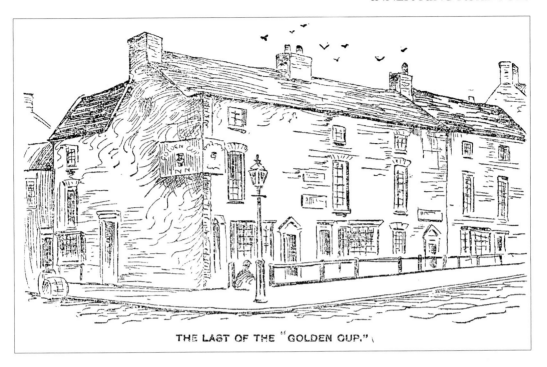

THE LAST OF THE "GOLDEN CUP."

The Golden Cup, Livery Street.

The Golden Cup, at 179 Livery Street, was an eighteenth-century public house built in the hollow of Livery Street, just beyond Snow Hill Station. The roadway was subsequently built up, giving the impression that the Cup had sunk 4ft or so. A separate path, railed off from the road, led down to it. Richard Duce was landlord from 1784. During his time the house was one of the meeting places of the Nightly Patrol Association, a group of prominent citizens who organised security patrols of the town. Duce died at the Golden Cup on 23 April 1803. His widow, Hannah, took over. Unfortunately in its latter days the Golden Cup had an unsavoury reputation, being the assembly place of the 'lounging and criminal fraternity', as one newspaper reporter described them, just after the Golden Cup closure in 1875.

At 19 Livery Street, in 1811, was the Turk's Head, run by Jane Emberton. Following her death, Richard Clark took over, and remained as landlord for thirty-eight years. This house closed in 1870 with the expiry of its lease. The Grapes at 42, opened post-1823. Jesse Sims was its first licensee. The Grapes temporarily relinquished its license in 1889 under landlady Mrs Mary Ann Evans, but it was re-issued on an annual basis up to 1892 when it was finally abandoned. The Crown & Anchor was situated two doors down from the corner of Northwood Street, on the western side of the road. It is first recorded as a named pub in the directory of 1818, with Elizabeth Hawkes listed as licensee. This public house closed in 1886.

The Shakespeare Tavern at 185 Livery Street originated in 1847-8, with Henry Weetman as its first known licensee. The house was rebuilt in 1892 to a design by Birmingham architect William Jenkins on a slightly larger area under the Improvement Scheme. It closed in 1915. Its number unknown, the George & Dragon was in existence by 1818. It closed in 1855, David Wollaston being its last licensee.

The original White Horse, Congreve Street.

The second White Horse, Congreve Street.

Congreve Street and Easy Row

The White Horse in Congreve Street was built in the late eighteenth century, at what was then 6 Friday Street. Its first licensee was Edward Glaze, listed in the trade directories from 1767 to 1777. Benjamin Jeavons followed him as landlord, and in 1815 William Holloway took over. In 1835 John Wells Carter became landlord. He was followed in 1845 by Christopher Yeomans, who in his advertisements described the White Horse as a 'Commercial and Market Inn'. He was followed by one of the pub's great characters, George MacDonald, affectionately known as 'Mac'. During Mac's tenure the White Horse gained a reputation as a theatrical house, and a recognised rendezvous of the company of the Theatre Royal. It was also the home of the original Birmingham Press Club (the oldest press club anywhere in the world). By 1861 Mac had been succeeded as landlord by fellow Scot, J. Blaclock. The new landlord began Burns' Night suppers at the White Horse, where the haggis was piped into the dining room. Another great landlord was Joseph Bailey, who introduced moderately priced lunches for local office workers. The daily Ordinary, as it was called, was served up at half past one, for the moderate charge of one and sixpence. At Christmas time it became Bailey's habit to provide a Boar's Head Dinner, free of charge, to his regular patrons. Bailey died in 1889.

John Westwood, the popular licensee of the Woodman, Easy Row.

115

The Woodman, Easy Row, 1962.

The Saloon Bar of the Woodman, December 1964.

In November 1905 the old premises were sold at auction, and bought by local brewers M&B. They demolished the old house and built a splendid new hotel on the site. The new White Horse was designed by Smethwick architects Wood & Kendrick. It opened in December 1907 under the management of Mr Edgar C.H. Oliver. In the sixty years that followed, the White Horse had only four managers, the last of whom was K.G. Haslewood, who was there for seventeen years. The White Horse closed on 30 June 1965 for the cutting of the now infamous Inner Ring Road and the construction of the equally execrable concrete bunker known as the Central Library.

There was a second, and earlier, public house along Congreve Street, the Johnson's Head. It was situated at 18 Congreve Street, on the corner of 58 Edmund Street. This public house was originally spelt 'Jonson' and took its name from the sixteenth-century playwright, Ben Johnson. Over the years an errant 'h' slipped in, and by 1860 the head had become that of Dr Samuel Johnson (1707-84), compiler of a Dictionary of the English Language. The Johnson's Head, under licensee, Samuel Tomlinson, became a coterie of the Tories of the town, known as the 'Church and King Party'. From here, it appears, the 1791 Priestley Riots were organised, resulting in the burning of houses and chapels of Nonconformists. William Tomlinson, Samuel's son, succeeded him as landlord, and after him came Charles Corbett and Joseph Whiles. With the increasing popularity of the White Horse nearby, the Johnson's Head went into decline. The last landlord was Charles Phipps, licensee from 1865 to 1870. The Museum and Art Gallery was later built on the site.

Above: *The Crown, Cherry Street, c. 1870.*

Left: *Suffield's Hotel, Union Passage.*

SUFFIELD'S HOTEL,

LUNCHEON BAR,

DINING & COFFEE ROOMS

UNION PASSAGE,

CONDUCTED IN THE BEST LONDON STYLE.

BILL OF FARE.—EVERYTHING IN SEASON.—CHANGED DAILY.

BASS' CELEBRATED ALES,

LONDON & DUBLIN STOUT. FIRST-CLASS SPIRITS.

Wines at New Tariff Rates.

ROOMS FOR LADIES. COMFORTABLE SMOKE ROOM. BEDS.

UNION PASSAGE, BIRMINGHAM.

Trade card for the Union Hotel, Union Street.

Trade card for the Union Hotel, Union Street.

The yard of the Union Hotel.

The Woodman quietly closed on New Year's Eve, 1964. It was the end of an era, as the cliché goes. There had been two pubs on this site, the first was an early nineteenth-century, plain and unadorned house opened in 1822 with Joseph Chirm as its first landlord. Before the building of the Council House, its smoking room was used as an informal meeting place for the town's Liberal councillors to discuss the government of Birmingham. For many years the landlord was Mr John Westwood, a tall, slim man of dignified appearance. In the evening he could generally be found occupying a corner seat, a tankard by his side. He was the son of Tom Westwood, landlord of the Nag's Head in Lichfield Street, and received his early training working for his father. Westwood succeeded to the Woodman on the retirement of his brother-in-law, Mr Jem Onions, in 1860. 'Father Frank', in Local Notes & Queries [1165] described his friend, John Westwood:

He was firm, yet gentle; polite, yet sincere; no lewd talk met encouragement from him. His parlour brought forth good thoughts and actions for the old town's benefit. Of such weight was the opinion of that parlour company that, at one time, it was said to rule the Town Council. In all good works John Westwood was a quiet helper; only a few weeks before his death I walked up Broad Street with him, and we talked of things of the past fifty years ago, and now alas, poor John Westwood is of the past too.

Westwood died in 1882. His widow, Fanny, continued to run the Woodman. In 1890 she sold up to Henry Mitchell jr, soon to link up with William Butler to form M&B. Mitchell decided to demolish the old house and build a new Woodman. Plans were drawn up by architect Henry Naden in 1891. The upper two storeys of the house he designed were plain enough. They were Northern Renaissance in style, and with just a hint of what was to come with a stone carving of a woodman with his dog above the front entrance. The ground floor was an extravaganza of carved wood and etched glass. There were two oriel windows with a central doorway, with two doors leading to two of its three bars. To the left oriel was a doorway leading to the public bar. The theme continued inside, with the added bonus of beautiful painted glass everywhere, including the snob screens in the Private Bar. There was a glorious profusion of decorated Minton tiles everywhere, while picture tiles upon the entrance passage walls by Albert Staton portrayed chapters in the city's history. In the year after its closure for the Ring Road, the tiles were saved, and placed in the Alhambra Bar in Hill Street.

Dwarfed by its neighbour above, the Queen's Arms was an unassuming little beerhouse in Easy Row. It was an early nineteenth-century house, updated in October 1886 by Henry Naden. The Queen's Arms closed in 1922.

Cherry Street and Union Street

Back across the city centre to Cherry Street and its continuation, Union Street. In Cherry Street was the Crown Tavern, a noted home-brew house in its day. The house is shown in the background of a view of the Wesleyan Chapel in Cherry Street, which appears in R.K. Dent's Making of Birmingham. It was a two-and-a-half-storey Georgian house of brick and tile. At one time it was the headquarters of the Birmingham Typographical Society, under landlord Jack Bootle. Its license was abandoned in 1881 under the Improvement Act.

The Street was originally a pathway from St Philip's church to Walker's Cherry Orchard. There was a public house here, alternatively known as the Bowling Green Tavern or the Golden Coffee Pot. Its owner at one time was Joseph Cooke, landlord from 1756 to post-1767, giving rise to this house also being known as Cooke's Tavern. The house had a large hall, or what was then termed a 'Great Room'. In February 1761 the local publicans were summoned here to discuss the repeal of a recently enacted rise in beer duty:

> The Publicans of this Town are desired to meet at Mr Cook's Great Room in the Cherry Orchard on Wednesday next the 18th Instant, at Two o'Clock in the afternoon, to consider of a proper Application to be made to Parliament for a Repeal of the late Act for laying an additional Duty upon Ale. As this is a matter of the utmost Consequence to Publicans in General and is thought necessary to apply before the Parliament breaks up which probably may be soon, it's hoped every one who conveniently can will attend.

In the late eighteenth century this tavern and its bowling green became the property of William Witherington, a surgeon at the General Hospital in Summer Street. He had the old house demolished, and a new home for himself built on the site.

The Coffee Pot in Cherry Street, taking its name from the house above, was a little beerhouse.

Extensions were carried out to it in 1888 by William Doubleday, with extra work carried out in the following year from plans submitted by James Moffatt on 4 September 1889. There was another beerhouse in Cherry Street, known as Taylor's. It only comes to light by name, when it was obliged to surrender its license in 1879 under the Improvement Scheme. One final house, the Gipsy's Tent, is listed in the trade directory of Birmingham for 1855 as being in 'Cherry Lane'. This would appear to be an error for Cherry Street. James Reading was its licensee.

Union Street and Union Passage leading off, were created when Corporation Street was cut through Cherry Street. The Stour Valley Hotel was at 40-1 Union Passage. It was opened by Joseph Suffield in 1852. By constant usage, it became known by the name of its founder, and had become Suffield's Bar. The license was temporarily surrendered to the Justices in 1883, but reinstated after the completion of Corporation Street. Owner E.A. Bird put forward plans for alterations to the house in December 1898. Suffield's narrowly escaped destruction during the Second World War, but in the post-war reconstruction of the site, now known as the Big Top (owing to the annual circus held here), it was included in the redevelopment scheme. Suffield's closed in 1960.

At 35 Union Passage was the Corner Luncheon Stores, a licensed victuallers opened in 1863 by Thomas Hanson. The legendry George Mountford managed it for a number of years. In the directory of 1937 its name is given as the Corner Cupboard, under licensee Horace West. The house closed in 1958 when Lower Bull Street and its vicinity were redeveloped. George Mountford later ran the Union Bar at 2 Union Street. He was one of the best known and most respected publicans in late Victorian Birmingham. Born in Worcester in 1846, he broke into the licensing trade as manager of Thomas Hanson's Corner Stores. Three years later Mountford purchased his own pub, the White Lion, in Bell Street. In 1873 he sold it in order to purchase the more prestigious Union Bar. He built up a clientele of socially well-to-do patrons. Mountford died in April 1893. In an obituary one reporter wrote:

> ... His dining room in Union Street was cribbed and narrow and always crowded at midday, and you found an extraordinary assortment of people there –- solicitors , bank clerks, auctioneers, doctors, commercial travellers, pugilists and pressmen. I have seen a solicitor of the Supreme Court of Judicature dining next to the ex-champion of the prize ring, and I have seen a prominent agent of the great Conservative party engaged in conversation with a well-known barrister. There were two points about the place – only men were admitted, and meat and drink were of the very best. A dandy who was taken there once was horrified to find that people dined there with their hats on, and he did not come near again for weeks, but he finally succumbed to the irresistible temptation, and was in the end one of its warmest supporters ... with genial, and often robust, manners with a certain class of his customers, he was always careful to be courteous and respectful to others. No one was allowed to call him by his surname alone. Intimates called him George, mere customers called him Mr Mountford. He never allowed people to call him Mountford.

Following his death, the license was taken up by Thomas Singleton, and Mountford's, as it was now popularly known, continued to provide lunches up until its closure in 1934.

The Union Inn, after which the street was named, opened on 4 May 1790. Edmund Goodbehere was its first landlord. The new inn was built very near the site of the old Golden Coffee Pot. Goodbehere advertised the opening of his new inn:

UNION INN AND TAVERN
Cherry Street, Birmingham
EDMUND GOODBEHERE having completely rebuilt the
Above INN and TAVERN, and added thereto some excellent
STABLING, begs Leave to acquaint the Public that he has
Fitted up and Furnished the same in a genteel Manner
With entire new beds, &c., for the particular accommodation
of GENTLEMEN TRAVELLERS, has laid in a stock of
rich Old Wines and other Liquors of the best Quality.
He therefore Solicit's the Patronage and kind Recommendation
of his Friends, which he will always endeavour
to merit by the most reasonable Charge and punctual
Attention to the Commands of his Customers. For the
Favours he has already experienced he thus publicly makes
His grateful Acknowledgments.

★★ An Ordinary at a Quarter past One, every Day, at one Shilling each.

After Goodbehere's death, his widow married a Mr Henry Birkett, a friend of her late husband, who held the license until 1799. He was succeeded by J. Price, Thomas Wells and Robert Bark, late of the Feathers in Ludlow. In 1825 the house was enlarged by licensee Robert Bark. A room was built over the gateway, and rooms were added-on in the yard. Under him the Union Hotel was used for meetings and public auctions. On a note of eccentricity, in its final days, the wife of one of its landlords always personally blew out all the candles as a sign that the bar was closing. By the time the last candle was blown out, all patrons should have quit the premises – otherwise they would have to feel their way in the dark to the door. The old inn was demolished in April 1879 under the Improvement Scheme for the cutting of Corporation Street.

The Cabin was tucked away off Bull Street, and approached down an entry. It was the sort of pub that you might discover by accident, having wandered down the alley out of curiosity. It was a tall mid-nineteenth-century building, altered over the fullness of time, with large windows, and in summer its entrance door was invariably propped open by a stool. It was an Atkinson's house, later taken over by M&B. The old Cabin closed in 1966 in preparation for the construction of the Inner Ring Road.

Edgbaston Street, Bell Street, Worcester Street and Phillips Street

The Bell Inn was a Markets' pub in Edgbaston Street, near its junction with Smallbrook Street. It was here that the Market Toll Book was kept. Turning to the page for August 1773 is the entry:

August 31, 1773. – Samuel Whitehouse, of the parish of Willenhall, in the county of Stafford, this day sold his wife Mary Whitehouse, in open market, to Thomas Griffiths, of Birmingham – value one shilling. To take her with all her faults.

(Signed) Samuel Whitehouse & Mary Whitehouse
Voucher, Thomas Buckley of Birmingham.

The Annual Register for that year, in which this event was recorded, revealed that: 'The parties were all exceedingly well pleased, and the money paid down as well for the toll as purchase.'

This was in the days when divorce was very costly, and could only be brought about by an Act of Parliament. Therefore this was a practical, and legal, solution. Some thirteen years earlier the Bell was featured in an advertisement in *Aris's Gazette* for 14 July 1760:

> A Society of Cricket Players of Birmingham would Play a Match there, the best of three Innings, with any others within 30 Miles of the Place, for 20 Guineas, and another Match for the like sum, at the Town from whence they may come. – Whoever chooses to accept this Challenge may apply to Thomas Bellamy, at the Bell in Smallbrook Street, Birmingham.

You would have to go a long away today to find such a pub; one where you could sell your wife, and have a good game of cricket too. Tragically the Bell Inn disappeared in the following century.

Down the other end of Edgbaston Street, near the Bull Ring, were two pubs side by side, the Old Crown Hotel on the corner with Lease Lane, and the Waggon & Horses next door. The Crown was in existence by 1553, where it is briefly mentioned in the Survey of Birmingham: '... the said tenement called the Crowne lies in Edgbaston Street...'. The house was rebuilt in the Georgian era. By 1835 it was known as the Old Crown. The brewers, Atkinson's, took it over in the late nineteenth century, to add to their stable of tied houses. R.F. Matthews was brought in to draw up plans for its alterations and updating on 24th February 1890. The front of the house was refaced in stone, with a mock balcony added on the first floor. Large windows were introduced on both frontages at ground level. This old house, there for nearly four hundred years, surrendered its license to the Justices in 1936.

The Waggon & Horses, next door, began life as the Reindeer. Built in 1702, it was an old three-storey house with bay windows either side of a central door. By 1755 it had become the Coach & Horses. John Crane was listed as licensee in the directory of 1767. John Hoffmeyer, a German clockmaker, took over the Coach & Horses in 1790. By the end of the Napoleonic Wars the house had been re-named the Waggon & Horses. George Ravenscroft updated the house in 1879, with further alterations and additions by architect Henry Naden from his plans of 14 August 1883. The Waggon & Horses was damaged during the Blitz in 1941, in the same raid that destroyed the old Market Hall. In the post-war era, its name now spelt with just one 'g', the Wagon & Horses stood there all forlorn, the buildings either side destroyed or cleared away, their sites boarded up. This old house closed in 1960 and was cleared away for the building of the 1963 Bull Ring Centre.

The Sydenham Hotel was on the corner of Edgbaston Street and Pershore Street. It began life as the Green Man, about 1817, under licensee William Carter. By 1855 it had become the Board, but by 1876 was closed and rebuilt as the Sydenham. Soon after, it was taken over by William Jones and renamed the Criterion. It was demolished in the 1960s for the construction of Smallbrook Queensway.

The Saracen's Head, sometimes referred to as the Turk's Head, was three doors up from Lease Lane. It was late seventeenth century in origin. There are early references to the house in the papers of the Governors of King Edward School. A mark of its national standing was the obituary of one of its former licensees, which appeared in the *Gentleman's Magazine* for July 1798:

The Crown and the Waggon & Horses, Edgbaston Street, 1924.

The Sydenham Hotel, Edgbaston Street, 1924.

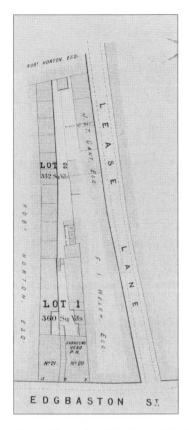

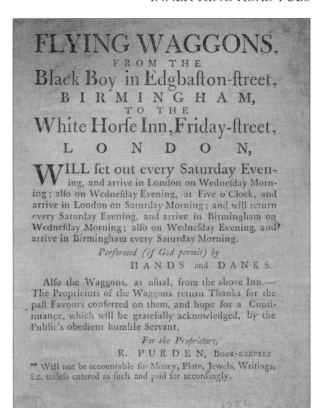

FLYING WAGGONS,
FROM THE
Black Boy in Edgbaston-ftreet,
BIRMINGHAM,
TO THE
White Horfe Inn, Friday-ftreet,
LONDON,

WILL fet out every Saturday Even-
ing, and arrive in London on Wednefday Morning; alfo on Wednefday Evening, at Five o'Clock, and
arrive in London on Saturday Morning; and will return
every Saturday Evening, and arrive in Birmingham on
Wednefday Morning; alfo on Wednefday Evening, and
arrive in Birmingham every Saturday Morning.
Performed (if God permit) by
HANDS and DANKS.

Alfo the Waggons, as ufual, from the above Inn.—
The Proprietors of the Waggons return Thanks for the
paft Favours conferred on them, and hope for a Conti-
nuance, which will be gratefully acknowledged, by the
Public's obedient humble Servant,
For the Proprietors,
R. PURDEN, Book-keeper.
☞ Will not be accountable for Money, Plate, Jewels, Writings,
&c. unlefs entered as fuch and paid for accordingly.

Above left: *A plan of the Saracen's Head, Edgbaston Street.*

Above right: *The Black Boy, Edgbaston Street, was a carriers pub.*

Aged 93, at a small cottage in the parish of Edgbaston, William Oram; who, more than 50 years ago, kept the Saracen's Head inn in Edgbaston Street, Birmingham. In the early part of life he was a porter to the London carriers at the Red Lion inn; and from his uncommon power in lifting heavy parcels, was deemed the strongest man in the town of Birmingham.

During the time of licensee James Street, in 1856, the house became the Old Saracen's Head. It became an Ansells tied house, closing in 1911.

The Black Boy was an old timber-framed house, whose name was later transferred to the Black Boy Inn in St Martin's Lane. The Widow Abney was landlady in 1767. She was followed as landlady by Mary Crane, licensee in 1782. The Black Boy closed in early 1796, and the site, advertised in the *Gazette* for April, was sold for development:

To be let for building, the land whereon the Black Boy Inn and buildings now stand, situate in Edgbaston Street, Birmingham. N.B. – That as the house adjoining the said inn will be taken down and a good opening made out of Edgbaston Street to communicate with the Warwick and Alcester roads for carriages this year, the above spot of land will be a very desirable one, either to erect an inn or other building upon.

THE

KING'S HEAD

FAMILY AND

Commercial Hotel,

*(Within Two Minutes' Walk of New Street Station, and Five
Minutes' of Snow Hill,)*

WORCESTER STREET,

BIRMINGHAM.

WILLIAM MUIR, PROPRIETOR.

ORDINARY EVERY DAY

At 1-15 p.m.

COMFORTABLE COMMERCIAL & LARGE STOCK ROOMS.

Families supplied with choice Wines & Spirits.

FIRST-CLASS BILLIARDS.

An advertisement for the King's Head, Worcester Street.

JACOB IN HIS UNIFORM.

*Jacob Wilson, the last Town Crier of Birmingham, was
landlord of the Bell.*

The Rose Inn, at 57 Edgbaston Street, was another old timber-framed house, whose history can be traced back to the seventeenth century. Thomas Fysher was listed as licensee in the Hearth Tax Returns of 1663. George Field was innholder between 1678 and 1681. The Rose was given a new frontage in the Georgian era. In its new guise it was a narrow-fronted house of three storeys, but stretching back for several rooms; with cast-iron balustrade atop a projecting square bay window onto its Edgbaston Street frontage. Its name was painted within a bricked-up window on the second floor, as is witnessed in an early 1930s photograph. The Rose surrendered its license on the 31 December 1934.

Anatomical pubs along the street include the Old King's Arms of 1767-77, the New King's Arms, also of 1767, the King's Arms, on the other side of Lease Lane from the Old Crown; the Nelson's Head of 1861, at 2 Edgbaston Street, and Boscowen's Head, named after Admiral Boscawen (1711-61). This pub was here during the 1760s and '70s. The King's Arms, referred to above, became the Chain, its front completely rebuilt in 1890 from plans drawn up by architect R.F. Matthews. The Falcon Hotel at 42, had John Hodgetts as landlord between 1767 and 1777, and the Golden Fleece was at 65 Edgbaston Street between 1818 and 1909. The York Hotel, at 15 Edgbaston Street, had Thomas Roberts as licensee between 1875 and 1881. Every pub mentioned was swept away by the 1950s with the building of the Bull Ring Centre. The Toreador was built as part of the new Bull Ring. Originally an Ansells house, it was taken over by Courage during the 1980s swap. It was closed for the building of the Millennium Bull Ring.

Proceeding up Spiceal Street from Edgbaston Street, the next road on the left was Bell Street. Undoubtedly the most famous public house here was the Leicester Arms, run by John Freeth. It was situated on the corner of Lease Lane. Under him it became more popularly known as the Coffee House or Freeth's Tavern. His father, Charles Freeth, formerly kept the Bell in Phillips Street, but had moved to the Leicester Arms by 1736. Under him the house had acquired a literary reputation; a reputation that the younger man maintained. Political writer, J. Morfitt, described Freeth in 1783:

John Freeth, the Birmingham bard, who 'writes songs, finds tunes, and sings them too,' is venerable for his years, respectable for his probity, and distinguished by home-spun wit and good humoured satire. He is one of the best political ballad writers and election poets in the kingdom.

Freeth also wrote about beer:

BIRMINGHAM BEER
Tune: 'Ye prigs who are troubled with conscience's qualms'.

Ye mortals who never, in all your wild trips
With good humming liquor saluted your lips
Give ear to my story, ye strangers to cheer,
The pleasure I sing of is Birmingham beer;
Then here ye Salopians, I beg you'd repair
If wonted to taste of the choicest of beer.

Our true orthodox, from the barrel fresh come
Throws the tankards lit up by the strength of the foam;
This strike-fire of nature, prepared right the dose,

Either 'livens or lulls to gentle repose;
'Tis the spring of invention, a balm that imparts
The cause that promotes and inspires us to arts;
Then who would not wish to partake of the juice
When knowing the feats it is wont to produce?

Let others in vain boast of different places;
But say, can they turn out such plump ruddy faces,
Such free jovial fellows, with cheeks red as roses?
Who swim in October to raddle their noses?
Ye beer-drinking souls, to good fellowship prone,
That dwell miles a hundred or more from our town,
'Tis well worth your notice among us to steer,
If only to taste of fam'd Birmingham Beer.

John Freeth died in 1808. His daughter Elizabeth took over the license and ran the Tavern for a number of years after. In later years the name of the Leicester Arms was changed to the Coach & Horses. This old tavern was demolished for the extension of the Wholesale Fish Market. Upon completion, on the opposite corner of Lease Lane, a new public house, the Grand Turk, was built to replace it.

The Grand Turk came into being around 1840, with William Moore as licensee. The next landlord, Joseph Page, is noted for having started up a horse omnibus service from Birmingham to Smethwick. The bus ran three times a day, including Sundays. Henry Smith took over in 1877. He remained there until 1899, a period of twenty-two years. The house survived the Blitz of 1941 that destroyed its near neighbour, the Market Hall, but was demolished for the construction of the 1960s Bull Ring Centre.

There had been a pub of a similar name in Bell Street, the Turk's Head at No. 26. It is first listed by name in the directory of 1799, with William Taft as its licensee. It closed in 1835 for the building of the Market Hall. Of curiosity was the Bill Posters Arms, a beerhouse under Tom Priest in 1837. There was the Sun, of 1767, and the Unicorn of 1796, and during the 1830s there was the White Lion, run by champion bare knuckle boxer, Bob Brettle. The Pump Tavern of 1790 had its name carried across the road to 8 Bull Ring when it closed in the 1830s. The Fleur-de-Lis, under Thomas Cooper, had been established by 1791, but likewise closed with the opening of the Market Hall. The Corn Market, a beerhouse, was here in 1840, with Richard Pickering as its landlord, and lastly there was the Butcher's Arms, at 6 Bell Street, from 1799 to 1818.

There is little or anything left of Worcester Street now. It linked Smallbrook Street and New Street. In its day it had over a dozen pubs at one time or another. There was a house called the King's Head which was demolished for the building of the Market Hall in 1834. The Seven Stars, just across the road at No. 73, under landlord Samuel Mayo, then took the name of the demolished house. The Seven Stars became the new King's Head. In 1852 it was offered for sale:

All that valuable and commodious HOTEL or COMMERCIAL INN, known as the KING'S HEAD, situated in Worcester Street, now in the occupation of Mrs Mayo, at a nominal rent; containing eleven bed Rooms, two Water Closets, large Sale Room and sitting Room, Coffee Room, Smoke Room, Spirits Shop, Bar, Kitchen, Back Kitchen, Brewhouse, and Malt Room, with excellent dry vaulted Cellars.

The house was sold to James Watson for £4,550. At the time it was listed at 63 Worcester Street. Though Watson was owner, Mrs Mayo remained as licensee of what soon after became the King's Head Railway & Commercial Hotel. The hotel closed in 1879-80 for extensions to New Street Station.

Thomas Parker was landlord of the Three Crowns, situated where the Market Hall was later built. He was here from 1807 until his death in September 1816. The Turk's Head was in existence by 1767, with the Widow Bayley listed as licensee. It closed in 1938. There was the Wine & Spirit Vaults of 1865, likewise the London & North Western Ale & Luncheon Stores of that same year. At 16 Worcester Street was John Wright's Coach & Horses of 1791, which closed in 1842. The Prince Eugene at 24, was in existence by 1785 under landlady Jane Short It was a public house favoured by bricklayers, who established a friendly society here. The Grand Turk was at 31 Worcester Street, built soon after the construction of the Market Hall, in 1835. The Oxford Hotel opened at Nos 41-42, in 1874, with Thomas Wells as licensee. One hundred years before, there was Hobson's Tavern at 47 Worcester Street. The bankrupt stock of Edward Noble was advertised for sale here, in the *Gazette* of 1782. Ann Hobson, widow of former licensee Thomas, was landlady at the time.

The New Market Tavern was at 50 Worcester Street. It took its name from the nearby Market Hall, opened in 1834. Thomas Harris was its first recorded landlord during the 1840s. The Tavern was given a new Victorian ground-floor frontage in 1869. It fell victim in 1908 to the 'fewer but better' policy of the City Council. Two doors up from the New Market Tavern was the Sportsman at 53. Near the junction of Worcester Street and Bell Street, it was opened in 1867. The last directory entry was in 1881. Originating a few years earlier, in 1877, was the Board, at 55 Worcester Street. In September 1883, architect William Jenkins oversaw renovation and updating. The Board closed in 1960 for the construction of the Bull Ring Centre. The Sun at 57 Worcester Street was an established house by 1796, when it was being run by John Dickenson. This house closed *c.* 1833. Lastly the Key Vaults at 85 Worcester Street opened in 1893 under landlady Mrs Emily Welch. Five years, and three licensees later, it closed, in 1898.

Linking Worcester Street and High Street, was Phillips Street, another casualty of the Inner Ring Road. The Bell, previously mentioned, was built in around 1710, and run by Charles Freeth during the following decade. In the early nineteenth century the Bell was bought by Jacob Wilson, the Town Crier. Alterations were carried out to the house in 1894 by W.H. Kendrick for owners Mitchell & Co. The Bell closed in October 1958 for the 1960s redevelopment of the Bull Ring. As well as the Bell, there was the Blue Bell, a mid-eighteenth-century Carriers house. Then there was the Golden Ball, established by 1767 under Joseph Newbury. The Fortunes of War was being run in 1767 by Jane Blackham. The house was closed post-1831 for the building of the Market Hall. The Old Cross, taking its name from the Market Cross in the Bull Ring, was established in the eighteenth century, Thomas Taylor was listed as a licensed victualler here between 1800 and 1812. He had formerly been landlord of the Old Crown in Deritend. The last licensee of the Old Cross was John Bragge in 1828. The White Swan, a beerhouse, would have gone totally unnoticed, but for an auction on 2 March 1870. It was described as:

A large and Commodius corner FREEHOLD PROPERTY in Phillips Street ... comprising the retail Public House, The White Swan, occupied by Mrs Mary Bushell, with gateway entrance, Brewhouse, Outbuildings and shopping over.

Beneath New Street Station

Peck Lane, Colmore Street, King Street, Queen Street and The Froggary, were all cleared away for the construction of New Street Station. Partially cleared were Old Meeting Street and the Old and New Inkleys. The most notable public house to disappear was Joe Lyndon's Minerva Tavern in Peck Lane. The house was situated on the corner with Queen Street, and had been a tavern from at least 1715. Its front had two large bow windows to the main level, with a flight of stone steps leading to the entrance door. The smoking room was the principal bar in house. It was a long narrow room with a low-beamed ceiling illuminated by its bow windows. Every morning, about eleven o'clock, free biscuits and cheese were placed on one of the tables for customers. This was the hour the merchants of the town frequented Lyndon's. These men of business conducted their affairs here in an informal atmosphere. The ale supplied and brewed on the premises had a wide reputation, especially the very potent Old Ale.

The Minerva was a Tory house, as opposed to the Whig house of 'Poet' Freeth on the corner of Lease Lane and Bell Street. About 1790, Freeth and his friends were advised that they and their political beliefs were not welcome at the house, and should they appear, would be summarily dealt with. A notice was put up over the fireplace – 'No Jacobin Admitted Here'. In defiance James Bisset, publisher of the Magnificent Directory of Birmingham, entered Lyndon's. Insults were traded, then one man blew smoke in Bisset's face. Up he got from his seat and knocked the man down. His friends reacted, and Bisset was thrown out through an open window into the street below. Many years after, Liberal politician George Edmunds was in Lyndon's when he got into a fierce argument with its Conservative clientele. He too was ejected through the self-same window, now christened 'Bisset's way out'. After Lyndon's death in August 1824, the trade fell away as one by one the old habitués died or moved away. In 1854 the house closed for the building of New Street Station.

There was a second public house, the Birmingham Inn, at 23 Peck Lane. It was in existence from 1767 until 1774 under licensee Richard Bowlker. At 13 Colmore Street, about one hundred yards from Joe Lyndon's Minerva Vaults, was the Eagle & Ball. The house possessed a large hall at the rear, and in 1778 the licensee, Joseph Warden, held singing evenings in here. In 1793 some of the regulars formed themselves into a friendly society known as the Anacreontic Society. Their first meeting was held on 24 October 1793. The society lasted for over twenty years. Its last member, William Marshall, was member 1,505. During the winter months there was constant discussion and entertainment. During the summer, amusement was provided by means of a marble alley. Within it was a circular disc of marbles, enclosed within a wooden collar. Here would come doctors, bankers, merchants and other respectable men to don knee-caps of stuffed leather, and on bended knee to try their skill at marbles. About 1839 Jem Onions took over the pub. He was well-liked, a man generally credited as of genial manner, a ready wit and well-informed. Soon the house became the rendezvous of thinkers, writers, musicians and respectable actors. With the coming of New Street Station the Eagle & Ball was closed. Onions moved to the equally pleasant Woodman in Easy Row.

There were two other public houses in Colmore Street. The Mermaid was in existence by 1818, under Joseph Beechgood, and the Jolly Malt-mill Maker of 1822, under John Kingham, which had evolved into the Malt Mill by 1841.

Vale Street, that once linked Navigation Street and the New Inkleys, was also a casualty of the railways. The Old Bull's Head, closed in 1881, was there in 1785, under licensee Robert Nechell. The King's Arms was at No. 9 from 1798, under first Richard Sill, then his widow, Elizabeth. The New Inkleys, off Hill Street, were also largely destroyed in the extension of New Street Station

The Market Hotel, 1924.

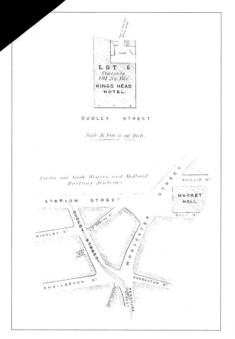

Plan of the King's Head, Dudley Street.

in the 1880s. At 10 New Inkleys was the Talbot, later renamed the Dog, dating from 1821, under Isaac Meyers. It closed in 1867. The Acorn was at 19 New Inkleys, and dated from 1823. It closed about the same time as the other two houses. At the Old Inkleys was the Bull's Head of 1800, under Ralph Williamson. He was followed by Thomas Perks, and then father and son, Samuel and Thomas Harfield, who were licensees here for forty years until the pub's closure in 1869. The Royal Oak was at 1 Old Inkleys from *c.* 1825 to the mid-1860s. Old Meeting Street, off Dudley Street, likewise suffered the loss of two pubs to the New Street Station extension. There was the Crown of 1767, under Joseph Hawkes, and the Lamp Tavern at No. 2, also dating from 1767. The survivor was the Goodfellows' Lodge at 4 Old Meeting Street, a house dating from post-1822. It was taken over by William Butler's Brewery in 1897, and updated. It finally closed in 1922.

Beak Street too was cleared for the station extension . There was one house here, the Lamp, on the corner of Cross Street. It first comes to light with the obituary of its first licensee, Charles Shuttleworth, in 1822. It had a further nine licensees before closing in 1869.

Queen's Street, though cleared for the construction of New Street Station, was later commemorated in the approach road to the station, Queen's Drive. Two pubs were demolished for the building of the original station, the Plume of Feathers and the Shakespeare's Head. The Plume of Feathers was at 39 Queen Street, and dated from 1828. The Shakespeare's Head at 14 Queen Street, was much earlier. William Morgan was listed as licensee in 1767. The pub closed in 1848.

If New Street Station was responsible for pubs closing, it was also responsible for new pubs and hotels opening. The Market Hotel on the corner of Station Street and Dudley Street was designed by Plevins & Norrington in 1883, and opened in 1884. It was built as part hotel, part warehouse, for pram maker Henry E. Jordan. The hotel was later taken over by Atkinson's Brewery, and in the 1950s it became an M&B house. Following a complete refurbishment within the last few years, its former grandeur has largely been restored. The hotel's public bar has been renamed Platform 13, a reference to the nearby New Street Station.

In Stephenson Street was the public bar of the Midland Hotel, which opened in 1878. Until 12 March 1970 it was a men-only bar – reputedly the last remaining in central Birmingham. The bar had an Edwardian quality about it, and was at its best at midday, being a favoured watering hole for professional and business men. The bar closed when the hotel closed for major refurbishment in the 1990s. Its replacement in the Burlington Hotel, as it became, was the Bacchus Bar. This is approached down a short flight of steps from the Burlington Arcade. The interior is perhaps a little over the top; a mixture of medieval baronial and Italian Renaissance. There was another bar attached to the hotel on the other side of the arcade, butting onto Stephenson Street. It was the Iron Horse, designed to resemble a railway carriage, the theme picked from its close proximity to the station. It had railwayana as décor. This bar closed when the hotel was redeveloped. Just across the road, but destroyed when the station was rebuilt in the 1960s, was the Queen's Hotel. It had a sizeable public bar, which opened in 1858 with W.J.B. Scott as licensee. The building next door was the Exchange, a Victorian meeting place for merchants and industrialists. Attached to it was a public bar and restaurant. The building, then one hundred years old, closed on 24 June 1965 for the rebuilding of the station. Incorporated in the new build was a new Exchange restaurant, initially known as the Berni Exchange. It was later renamed the Slug & Lettuce, the name that it operates under today. More or less facing the Iron Horse was the Gilded Cage, a disco pub, which opened on 3 December 1970. The pub contained a dance area, large enough to allow a dozen couples to dance. It was very Seventies. Unfortunately a few years later its subdued lighting attracted drug dealers. Subject of a number of police raids, it was closed down. It reinvented itself, with brighter lights, but closed again, this time permanently. On the central concourse of New Street Station, beyond the ticket barrier, is the 1960s Taurus Bar, formerly the Station Bar. It is a free house.

Dudley Street has now largely disappeared. The King's Head at No. 55 consisted of a 'large and handsome Spirit Vaults, Smoke Room, Billiards Room, fifteen Chambers, and ample Business and Domestic Accommodation', as a notice of its sale in 1899 reveals. Its first known licensee was William Belcher. He, his wife Ann, their son Robert and his wife, ran the King's Head Tavern for forty years. The house closed in 1894. The curiously named Half Moon & Seven Stars was in existence by 1811. Esther Savage was licensee. By 1817 the name had been truncated into the Half Moon. The pub closed in 1864. There were three eighteenth-century houses here, listed in the trade directory of 1767: the Blue Ball, under landlord, Edward Greazley, the Star, at 38 Dudley Street, with John Matthews as licensee, and the Salutation with William Hodgkinson. Of curiosity in Dudley Street was the Box Inn, a beerhouse, drawn to our attention with the obituary of its licensee, William Lucock, on 15 April 1805. The little-known Refreshment House, a beerhouse, had its license withdrawn by the Justices in 1924. The Bell, being a beerhouse, likewise is not recorded in Kelly's Directories of Birmingham. It comes to light with an obituary account for one of its licensees, Thomas Butcher, on 14 October 1805. Five more public houses remain in Dudley Street. The Royal Exchange, at 21, opened in 1869 under Alfred Bradbury. It appears to have closed in 1882. Also closed that same year was the Leicester House at 14 Dudley Street. It opened in 1870. Zachariah Gilbert was its first licensee. The Railway Guard of 1860, under Edward Roberts at 52, suffered the ignominy of being turned into a shop in 1866. The Apple Tree, at 63 Dudley Street, a three-storey late eighteenth-century house on the corner of Edgbaston Street, was acquired by the Ashted Brewery in 1881. It too has now gone. Finally the Bull's Head, on the corner of Great Queen Street, opened in 1854, and closed for station extensions in 1878.

Smallbrook Street

In September 1873, one Mr Cohen, of the Stores, at the junction of Smallbrook Street and Tonk Street, applied to the Justices for a full license. He had the backing of many well-known local figures, including the historian and writer, Samuel Timmins. The licensing Justices pointed out that the neighbourhood was well provided for, with one public house for every twenty-eight yards. These included the Black Lion at 20 Smallbrook Street, dating back to *c.* 1820, and originally known as the Golden Cross. The change of name took place in 1830. Narrowly escaping the Blitz, during the Second World War, it was situated in a block of five narrow-fronted terraced houses. An Atkinson's house, it closed in 1956 and was demolished for the cutting of Smallbrook Queensway. The Red Lion was at No. 20. It was there by 1767, under John Chapman, landlord until 1775. It closed in June 1959 for the construction of the Ring Road. The Golden Eagle at No. 49 dated from *c.* 1865, under licensee James Smith, and the Black Swan (No. 61), was hatched about 1822. The Licensing Justices withdrew its licence on 28 December 1934. From the same nest came the White Swan (No. 73), established by 1789 under William Ward. The house had closed by 1845.

The Bull's Head was at the corner of Smallbrook Street and the Horsefair. Established by 1825, it was at one time known as the Bull's Head Liquor Vaults. Under William Clucas the house expanded into the Horse Fair by the purchase of neighbouring buildings. The Bull's Head was bought up by Cheshire's Brewery of Smethwick and rebuilt to the designs of James & Lister Lea, re-opening in 1894. The *Caterer & Hotel Keepers' Gazette* for 15 November 1894 described the new premises:

> In the place of the old inn has sprung up an elegant hotel... The elevation is most imposing...
> Consideration for patrons' comfort is shown in every way ... throughout the fittings care has
> been taken that everything should be in good taste and harmony.

It was a very impressive three-and-a-half-storied building of red brick and terracotta, with large plain glass windows on the ground floor. It was a building that dominated that corner, with a domed tower above its corner entrance. Another victim of the Inner Ring Road, the Bull's Head was replaced by the Jester, a very modest M&B house, with a jester motif on its polished stone front, and London-style central bar inside.

Facing the Bull's Head was the Malt Shovel at 48-51 Smallbrook Street, a rambling and many-doored establishment. It is first recorded as a public house in the trade directory of 1767. John Meer was its licensee up to his death in 1791. The Malt Shovel took over 50 and 51 Smallbrook Street in the 1830s under John Smith. While minor alterations were undertaken, there was no major rebuild. In the end it simply could not compete with the new Bull's Head across the road. The Malt Shovel closed in 1902, its license transferred to the newly built Argyle.

The Argyle, at 50 Smallbrook Street, was a four-storied Edwardian red-brick building situated at the junction of Suffolk Street and Holloway Head, facing onto the Horse Fair. A very elegant building, it was built for the Holt Brewery and opened in 1902 with Albert Henningham as its first licensee. During the 1920s part of the ground floor was sold off and converted into a branch of the Westminster Bank. The site was compulsorily purchased by the City's Traffic Control Committee in October 1929 and demolished in June 1930 as a road improvement scheme.

The Golden Cup is the earliest known of Smallbrook Street's public houses. It was advertised for sale in 1751:

The Jester, Smallbrook Queensway.

The Argyle, junction of Suffolk Street and John Bright Street, 1924.

The Malt Shovel, Smallbrook Street, 1870.

To be Lett, and entered upon immediately, or at Christmas next, the Old Golden Cup, situated in Smallbrook Street, Birmingham; being an old-accustomed Mug House.

A hundred years later, then licensee of the Golden Cup, John Swann, opened a small music hall here, which he called the Royal Standard Concert Room. By the time the next licensee, William Haddleton, had taken over, in 1859, the concert hall had been abandoned. The Golden Cup closed in 1865.

Other early beer and public houses here include the Saracen's Head of 1767 under Thomas Farr, and the Horse & Jockey of the same date under George Naiden. Of slightly later date was John Perkes' Lamp Tavern of pre-1790. A quick dash through some of the other public houses in Smallbrook Street includes: the Eagle & Child of 1818, with Samuel Hodgkinson as licensee;

139

the Little Gem of 1880, with William Howes; the Crown at 29 Smallbrook Street, in existence from 1822 to 1830; the Cross (No. 20), opened in around 1833 under George Davis and closed in 1866; the Macready (No. 37), named after actor-manager William Charles Macready (1793-1873), opened in 1854 but gone by 1858; and the Three Tuns at 13 Smallbrook Street. It dated from 1827, with William Adams. The house survived until 1959, when it was closed for the Inner Ring Road. There were four music hall bars: the Crystal Palace, run by James Day in 1854; the Era run by Harry Day from 1869; the Theatre of around 1838, run by David Levi; and lastly the Empire Vaults of 1895 to the early 1960s, closed for the Inner Ring Road.

With the completion of the Inner Ring Road, new pubs were built along Smallbrook Ringway. They include, beneath the Rotunda, the Mulberry Bush, one of the two pubs that were bombed by the IRA in November 1974. Rebuilt, it was renamed the Roundabout, and later Bar St Martin. It was demolished for the construction of the Millennium Bull Ring Centre. The Viking, an M&B house, was situated not far from the old Rep Theatre, and was a favoured house for theatre staff. The Wandering Minstrel was in the West Court of the Bull Ring Centre, a little way back from the Queensway. Another M&B house, it opened on 27 May 1964. In its latter years its name changed nearly every weekend to try and catch a dwindling clientele. It became 49ers, M&Ms, Peacocks, Genesis, and Emma's Bar. In June 2000 it was put out of its misery and demolished for the new Bull Ring Centre. The Horse Trader, another 1960s pub, was an Ansells house. Like the other '60s pubs it changed its name once or twice, until in the end you became confused about the names – Blueberry's? O'Rafferty's? Who cared? They were of their time – and their time had gone.

Tonk Street is now the lower part of Hill Street at its junction with Smallbrook Street. There were two houses here, the Sign of the Compasses, a beerhouse, briefly acknowledged in an obituary of its licensee, one 'Warley', in February 1807, and the General Elliott, of interest because in 1855 its licensee, Joseph Hobson, appeared before the Birmingham Quarter Sessions of 25 June 1855. He was charged with having received a stolen £50 note, the property of one Frederick Omber. Found guilty, he was sentenced to be transported to Australia, probably one of the last Englishmen to be so sentenced. The General Elliott closed in 1894.

Suffolk Street

Suffolk Street now forms the western boundary of the Inner Ring Road, and is known as Suffolk Street Queensway. The King's Arms at 14 Suffolk Street was a former home-brew house on the corner with Hinckley Street. It opened in about 1838, Isaac Moore being its first licensee. It was taken over by Holder's Brewery, and added to their stable of eighty-three tied houses. In 1891 the pub was bought by William Jones, and extended fairly considerably under architect William Jenkins, from plans drawn up by him on 4 August 1891. The house was renamed the Criterion, the name it bore until its closure in 1925.

The first authenticated reference to the Wheatsheaf at 43 Suffolk Street is in 1808. Its first known licensee was Paul Gardner. A former home-brew pub, it was acquired by Mitchell's Brewery around 1891, bringing the brewery's stable of tied houses up to eighty-six. In 1898 the company merged with William Butler's Crown Brewery of Broad Street to become M&B. In the following year, 24 March 1899, Smethwick architects Wood & Kendrick drew up plans for the Wheatsheaf's updating. This old house, by then over 150 years old, closed in 1960 for the construction of the Suffolk Street section of the Inner Ring Road.

The doorway of the King's Arms, Suffolk Street, c. 1902.

The public house at 52 Suffolk Street was renamed four times. Situated at the top of Suffolk Street, not far from the canal basin, it began life as the Boat in 1780, under licensee Richard Ashford. Thomas Brooks, the miller at Chapman's Windmill, at nearby Holloway Head, bought the house in 1840 and renamed it the Millwright's Arms. He ran it for six years before selling up to John Hadley, who promptly renamed it the Castle. Barely two years later, Hadley changed his mind, and reverted back to the house's original name of the Boat. About 1886, landlord James Johnson, changed the name again, this time to the Midland Inn. Architect William Hopkins was brought in to update it in June 1895. The house closed in May 1922. The Red Lion at 63 Suffolk Street was situated midway between Swallow Street and Navigation Street, across the road from Worcester Wharf Goods Station. It appears to have originated post-1825. Thomas Southall was landlord here from 1828 to 1872, a period of forty-four years. Frederick Hughes was landlord in 1892, when the Red Lion closed.

The Blue Bell, a public house dating from 1796, was at 79 Suffolk Street. Under licensee Charles Rainsford the house became the Bell Spirit Vaults. It returned to its original name when David Clift took over in 1859. The Bell closed in 1882. At 88 Suffolk Street was the Dolphin, of 1822. The house became the Old Dolphin under landlady Mary Smith. In 1878, landlord William Wright commissioned architect Charles J. Hodson to update the house according to his plans of 3 August. Less than six years later, in 1884, the Dolphin was forced to close when the land was required for the construction of the Midland Railway Goods Depot.

Architect William Jenkins prepared plans on 10 February 1878 to update the British Oak at 101 Suffolk Street. The house had opened in 1853 with William Hartland as licensee. It closed in 1887. The Rising Sun was at 108, on the western side of the road near its junction with Severn Street, and almost opposite the Wheatsheaf. It opened in 1800, but, being a beerhouse, was not listed by name in the directories of the day. There is a very brief death notice for one 'Mason', its licensee, who died on 11 November 1800. The Rising Sun closed in 1889, following the termination of its ground lease. The Plough was situated at 128 Suffolk Street, on the corner with Gough Street. It originated c. 1845 and closed in 1907.

Other pubs and beerhouses here include the Sign of the Fish, originating in 1797 and closing c. 1815. Then there was the Bricklayers Arms of 1827-32, on the corner of Gough Street, and the Old Bricklayers Arms, a much earlier house, dating from 1818. There was the Chequer, used as a salesroom for barley, in 1809, and the Punchbowl, of the same date. The Three Crowns was on the corner of Wharf Street, up near Broad Street, run by Irishman Frank MacKaness post-1812. It closed in 1884. The Old Red Lion Spirit Vaults was demolished for the building of the Technical School in 1893. The Fifth Public House originated in 1784 under William Savage. He was there until 1795. Then there was the Grapes, a public house at the junction of New Inkleys. It was there in 1868; its lease expired in March 1887. Of the new boys, originating in the 1990s, there is After Dark and the Circo Bar. Perhaps if they survive long enough they will develop character too.

Paradise Street

Public houses in Paradise Street, and beyond it, Paradise Place and Forum, date from the 1780s. There was the Crispin, in existence from around 1785 to the death of its licensee, William Phillips in November 1788. There was the Rose & Crown, of similar date, under George Parley, and of slightly later date, the Navigation. Ten canal narrow boats were sold here at auction,

The King's Arms, Suffolk Street, 1924.

HENRY SMITH,
'WHEAT SHEAF',
And Commercial Inn,
SUFFOLK STREET, BIRMINGHAM.
TWO MINUTES' WALK FROM THE NEW STREET STATION.

Choice Wines and Spirits direct from the Docks.

An advertisement for the Wheat Sheaf, Suffolk Street.

The Wheatsheaf, Suffolk Street, 1924.

Bread & Roses, formerly the Grape Vine, Paradise Forum.

according to the *Birmingham Gazette* of 10 October 1791. The White Hart was a three-storied Georgian building dating from 1803. Francis Twist was its first licensee. The house was acquired by Butler's Brewery in 1897 (later M&B), who updated it with an impressive Art Nouveau front with a wood-framed and leaded glass entrance. In 1951 the White Hart extended sideways into the former premises of J. Rousell Ltd. This house closed on 15 August 1965, being the last of a small group of public houses including the nearby Hope & Anchor and the White Horse in Congreve Street, which had closed during the week of 22 to 27 June 1965 for the development of the Inner Ring Road and the building of the new Central Library.

Replacement post-Inner Ring Road pubs include the Grape Vine, as part of the Central Library development of 1973. The house had a makeover and a new name in the 1990s. In 2003 however its lease fell due, and was not renewed. The pub was taken over by the trade union, Unison, on a nine-year lease from Birmingham City Council. It was renamed Bread & Roses. The venture failed in late May 2004, after fifteen months of trading, leaving the union with losses of £120,000. The house re-opened not long after as the Stage, and is now run successfully by the owners of the Prince of Wales in Cambridge Street.

Within the later glazed Forum beneath the library, a number of shops and bars were built, including Raphael's and Hooters Bar. While Raphael's became the unofficial home of the Dutch fans during the 1996 European Cup held in England, Hooters went into decline. It closed in 1999. The site was acquired by the Weatherspoon chain, refurbished at a reputed cost of £700,000, and opened on 1 February 2001 as the smallest of the chain's pubs. Beneath the library, Notes opened in 1987, following the construction of the nearby ICC and the regeneration of Broad Street. The name of the pub is taken from the nearby School of Music. An illuminated golden saxophone is featured on its outside wall.

Pinfold Street

Pinfold Street takes its name from the pinfold or penfold, where stray cattle were rounded up and kept until reclaimed by their owners. Perhaps appropriately at 36 Pinfold Street was the Dun Cow. An eighteenth-century beerhouse, it is named in the directory of 1818. It closed about 1845. There were three un-numbered public houses in Pinfold Street dating from the late eighteenth century. The Hercules was listed in the 1767 trade directory of Birmingham; the Red Lion comes to light as an obituary entry for Benjamin Jukes, who died on 6 July 1797, and the Bell is featured in the 1785 directory, with Richard Newbury as landlord. Up on the corner with Paradise Street at 1 Pinfold Street was the Coach & Horses, right next door to Joe Hillman's Stores. In fact at the weekend, when the Stores was closed, many of the staff worked at the Coach & Horses. The house was in existence by 1848. William Dennis carried out additions to the house in February 1886. Both the Coach & Horses and the Stores were closed for the building of the General Post Office in Victoria Square.

At 56 Pinfold Street was the Blucher, named in honour of Field Marshall Blucher, Prussian Allied Commander at the Battle of Waterloo. The house was opened post-1815, but is not identified by name until 1823, so it is probable that it was only a beerhouse before this date. It closed about 1843. At 60 Pinfold Street was the Elephant & Castle, taking its name from the coat of arms of the city of Coventry. Its licensee between 1767 and 1774 was Job Baker. There are no further entries for the Elephant & Castle after 1823, and it appears to have been renamed the Bull's Head. Its first recorded licensee was Mary Lloyd. Her successor was John Aspinall, who was landlord for twenty-five years until the Bull's Head's closure in 1852. Lastly there was the Three Tuns at 66 Pinfold Street. Seemingly a beerhouse in origin, there is an obituary in the *Gazette* for one-time licensee Joseph Wilkes, who died on 2 January 1823. By 1827 the Tuns had a full license, and the house is listed by name with Joseph Harding as landlord. Edward Gold bought up the house, and was licensee here until its closure in 1844.

Navigation Street

The Greyhound Inn at 27 Navigation Street began life as the Man Loaded with Mischief in 1779, under licensee John Woodcock. He adopted Hogarth's celebrated picture as his inn sign. The sign was copied by Richard Wilson, better known as a white clock dial painter, and attracted such crowds that the Magistrates were called in and ordered its removal. The house was renamed the Stag's Head, and shortly after was taken over by John Porter, a former coal dealer. When he retired, George Garner, a diesinker, took up the tenancy. Unfortunately when trade fell off, Garner reverted to his original trade, and turned his hand to coining. Discovered and brought to trial, his sentence of capital punishment was commuted to one of transportation to Australia. The next landlord at the Stag's Head was Edward Harcourt, who in order to remove the stigma from the house, renamed it the Greyhound. In 1838, John Southall, a former teacher, took up the tenancy. A man of culture, Southall instigated the Musical Society and the Apollo Glee & Friendly Society. Musical concerts were held on Saturday evenings, and it was here that the great English tenor, Vernon Rigby first appeared. Among the Greyhound's regulars was the landscape artist, David Cox, and the millionaire pen manufacturer, Joseph Gillott.

Southall remained as licensee for over forty years, and in time the Greyhound was alternatively known as 'Southall's'. At the age of seventy-five Southall handed over the running of the pub to his son in 1877. The Greyhound was pulled down in 1909 for an extension to the Municipal Technical School.

The nearby Hope & Anchor was a political house. It became known for its Sunday evening debates on topical subjects of the day, and was the informal home of the newly emergent Liberal Party. John Bright and George Dixon were amongst the MPs who debated here. Perhaps its most influential and popular landlord was Robert Edmunds, licensee for over thirty years. Apart from originating the debating society, he also established a sick club, in the days before the Welfare State, and an 'Artisans' Penny Fund', with money going to support the Queen's Hospital. The Hope & Anchor also held musical nights, where singers obliged the company with a song or recitation. Among the favourite singers was local man Vernon Rigby, who later went on to national acclaim. This delightful old pub was compulsorily purchased in 1886 by the Midland Railway and demolished to make way for the extension of New Street Station.

The Nag's Head was the political precursor to the Hope & Anchor. The Hampden Club held its meetings here after its removal from the Saracen's Head in Snow Hill. These meetings eventually led to the Political Union of the 1830s and the agitation for the establishment of Members of Parliament for Birmingham. The White Swan was at 26-7 Navigation Street, just across the road from the Greyhound Inn, and dated from 1817. Alterations and additions to the house were undertaken by John Hopkins in 1886 and William Jenkins in 1896. The house was pulled down for extensions to New Street Station. A second White Swan was later opened as a replacement, but it was forced to close in the 1960s for the redevelopment of the station. Situated on the other corner of Navigation Street and Summer Street was the Acorn. The house

An obituary for Robert Edmonds, licensee of the Hope & Anchor.

dated from 1807, when it is named in landlord William Danks' obituary. He himself is listed as a victualler here from 1786. Architect George Ravenscroft undertook alterations to the Acorn from his plans of 29 October 1878. The house closed in 1881 with the extension of New Street Station.

Harris' Public House, its name probably derived from a former licensee, is featured in the obituary of 'Mrs Hodgetts', the widow of former landlord Charles Hodgetts, licensee from 1803-12. The Roebuck was at 27 Navigation Street and opened to the public between 1828 and 1835 under John Stokes. There is just one known reference to the Vine, at 88 Navigation Street; that is the trade directory entry of 1861, when Thomas Beach was listed as licensee. The Mogul was a beerhouse in Navigation Street. It is noted in an obituary of landlady Mrs Badham, who died on 5 February 1805. The Country Girl first opened in 1797, Joseph Dale was licensee from then up to 1812. His widow Ann took over and she was followed by Robert Williams. Like many other public houses in Navigation Street, it fell victim to the expansion of New Street Station, and closed in 1867. The White Lion at 46 Navigation Street originated *c.* 1820, with Edward Chambers as licensee. He was followed by John Smallwood, landlord for twenty-seven years. John Powell was its last licensee, landlord for thirteen years until the White Lion's closure in 1884. The last of the known public houses here was the Swan (Luncheon Bar), at No. 79. A licensed victuallers, situated on the corner of Summer Street, it was in existence by 1796, as an advertisement of that year relates. The Swan closed in 1932.

Fordrough Street was situated at the western end of Navigation Street. At 27 Fordrough Street was the Box Inn, dating from 1827. William Reeves was its first licensee. Later licensee, William Shaw, was landlord for twenty-nine years, from 1832 to 1861. The Box Inn closed in 1871.

Left: *The Hope & Anchor, Navigation Street.*

Below: *The Swan Luncheon Bar, Navigation Street.*

SWAN LUNCHEON BAR,
NAVIGATION STREET.

PROPRIETORS—E. J. SWIFT & Co.   MANAGER—R. W. J. OSMOND.

DINNERS DAILY 12-30 UNTIL 2

HOLDERS' ALES & STOUT.   E. J. SWIFT & Co.'s WINES & SPIRITS.

"Swan" Musical Society meets every Saturday evening at 8 p.m.
Chairman—J. OWEN.

John Bright Street

John Bright Street, situated at the junction of Navigation Street and Hill Street, was cut in 1881 at a cost of £31,000. The road was driven through the worst of the surviving slums of central Birmingham.

At its Suffolk Street end it followed the route of the New Inkleys, likewise swept away. The Queen's Tavern, at 39 New Inkleys, opened in 1853, with Charles Hobbins registered as its licensee. In 1883 the license was temporarily suspended when the house was totally rebuilt. The new Victoria, as it was named, at 48 John Bright Street, on the corner with Station Street, was designed by Thomas Plevins, and opened in 1884. Thomas Heatley was its first manager. The Victoria was taken over by William Butler's Crown Brewery in 1890, and in the following year alterations and updating was assigned to well-known pub architect William Jenkins. The ground floor was altered again in 1908 by architects Watson & Johnson. The Victoria subsequently became an M&B tied house. Today it is popular with the staff of the nearby Alexandra Theatre, and the theatre's patrons.

Hill Street

The Golden Eagle stood on the corner of Hill Street and Swallow Street in one form or another for over 206 years. The original house was an end terrace house, depicted though not named on Thomas Hanson's Plan of Birmingham for 1778. The Golden Eagle was first named in the Birmingham directory of 1829. Joseph Wasdell was its landlord. Its address was given as 49 Swallow Street. Wasdell died at the age of forty-seven on 19 March 1842. In an 1870 drawing of Hill Street, the Golden Eagle is shown as a three-storey house with a corner doorway and a large lantern above the door. Alterations and updates were carried out to the house in 1878 by architect Charles Brook Dobson, and in 1888 by William Horton. Taken over by Ansells, the old house was pulled down, and a new Golden Eagle, designed by Frank J. Osborne, was built in 1935. The ground floor of the Eagle was faced in polished black granite, above the corner entrance was a very Germanic-looking golden eagle. During the 1970s and '80s, the large upstairs assembly room was used for live music at the weekends. The Golden Eagle closed on 5 January 1984 for the redevelopment of the area. For a decade or so previously it had been a bikers' pub, so naturally the various bikers groups descended on their old stomping ground for a last nostalgic drink. Unfortunately words were exchanged, and a riot broke out. At the end of the night the pub itself was badly damaged; there was blood and skin all over the place, four customers were arrested for being drunk and disorderly, and one policeman was sent off to hospital with a suspected broken nose. Its replacement was the more up-market Henry's, built a few years later, a little further up the hill. It was situated in an interesting new build on the corner of Paradise Street and Hill Street. Henry's adopted an Art Nouveau décor, right from its entrance lamp, very Paris Metro in concept, right throughout the building. It was high Victoriana, with little embellishments that showed that someone had made an effort in its creation. The original entrance lamp has now gone, and the house has been renamed Victoria's.

Further down, on the other side of the road, was the Horse & Jockey at 13 Hill Street. It was established in 1822 by Thomas Greensill. In 1875 the house was renamed Sir John Barleycorn, soon shortened to John Barleycorn. The house closed in 1883. At 14 Hill Street, in the previous century, was the Saracen's Head. In existence by 1767, John Bolton was listed as its licensee.

Right: *The Victoria Inn, on the corner of Station Street and John Bright Street, 1924.*

Below: *A contemporary view of the Victoria.*

He was followed from 1773 by John Hardman. He established a building society here as an advertisement in *Aris's Gazette* for 5 February 1776 relates. Hardman died on 23 August 1810. Five more licensees followed at the Saracen's Head, before its closure in 1842.

At 23 Hill Street was the Bull's Head, of 1823, under James Cottrell. It briefly became the Theatre in 1852-3, with Adam Uriah Bryant as landlord. In 1855 it was renamed the Star & Garter under incoming owner and licensee James Price. This house closed in 1870. Nearby on the corner of Hill Street and 13 Cross Street was the short-lived beerhouse, the Swan & Railway of 1855, under George Stainton. At 35 Hill Street was the Jolly Bacchus, an early nineteenth-century public house established by 1822, which closed about 1842. At 45 Hill Street was Tonk's Hotel, taking its name from John Tonks. It opened in 1859, but had closed by 1862.

Of boxing interest was the Sampson & Lion, at 46 Hill Street. Jabez White, a former Birmingham boxer of national repute, kept the house from 1911 to 1914. The Sampson & Lion is first recorded one hundred years earlier in 1811. John Atkins was its first known licensee. In 1883, the Staffordshire brewers Fox & Co. bought the house, but it was later taken over by Ind Coope & Co. The Sampson & Lion surrendered its license in 1936.

The Rodney at 51 Hill Street was opened by William Harper in 1821. He was a plater by trade. The house first appears by name in Pigot's Directory of 1828. In 1882, nearby slum Green's Village was demolished for the cutting of John Bright Street, and so too was the old Rodney. The Derby House in Hill Street lost its license about this time, though it had not been scheduled for demolition. The house was purchased by the well known and highly respected publican George Mountford in 1885, and he succeeded in having the Rodney's license transferred to the Derby House. On the approval of the Licensing Justices, he reopened the house as the Hill Street Stores.

The Falstaff, at 72 Hill Street, originated in 1812 under Henry Taylor, whose obituary appears in the *Gazette* for 26 May 1823. He was followed by Joshua Knight, landlord for sixteen years, who, on retiring, was succeeded by Elizabeth and Mary Grundy. The house closed about 1845. The Lord Hill was at 103 Hill Street. It was named after Rowland Hill (1772-1824), Lord of Hawkstone, second in command at the Battle of Waterloo. The Lord Hill originated *c.* 1817. It had two known licensees, Thomas Linton and Walter Grosvenor. It was taken over by Edward Tidman, *c.* 1831 and renamed the Unicorn. It closed in 1870.

Also at 103 Hill Street, but only after some street renumbering, was the Jim Crow. The pub was named after an American Negro minstrel. This pub in Hill Street, not far from the notorious Green's Village, developed a reputation as a bit of a thieves den, and place of low repute. It closed apparently on the recommendation of the police, *c.* 1871.

Two short-lived houses in Hill Street: the Artillery Man of 1818, run by James Martin, and the Bacchus run by James Doughty from 1812 to 1818. The Acorn, on the corner of Hill Street and Cross Street, later renamed Severn Street, had a bewildering number of addresses due to redevelopment in the area. A casualty of the Blitz, it closed in 1941.

The Grapes at 78 Hill Street originated in 1840, Samuel Sims was its first landlord. The house was acquired by the Manchester Brewery Co. Ltd in 1898, who were later taken over by Ansells. Under them the old house was demolished, and a new house built to the design of John P. Osborn & Son in 1938. It was three storeys in height and faced in a combination of block and slab terracotta. The completed pub was featured in the *Brick Builder* for September 1938. Visually the Grapes was very similar to Osborn's other Hill Street pub, the Golden Eagle. The Grapes closed in 1964, and was rebuilt to a much plainer design. By the 1980s the house was looking a little seedy. It was extensively refurbished, and re-opened as Hill Street Q's, a development devoid of character. It had become a large room. In September 2005 the pub closed and became a mini-mart.

Left: *Henry's, Hill Street, now renamed Victoria's.*

Below: *Hill Street Q's, Hill Street, has now become a mini-mart.*

OPENING TOMORROW NIGHT!

THE
ALHAMBRA BAR

at the Savoy,
Hill Street, Birmingham

Authentic Victorian Decor
Music by
Brian Fine & Bryan Dandy!

Star Appearance
LIBBY MORRIS *on Saturday Night!*

Enjoy your favourite
BASS, MITCHELLS & BUTLERS BEERS
and Special Low Cost Lunches

———— ✳ ————

Good Simple Food:
SAUSAGES & MASH · SHEPHERD'S PIE
EMPRESS OF INDIA CURRY

Go along to the Alhambra and have fun!

Above left: *The Malt Shovel, corner of Hill Street and John Bright Street, 1924.*

Above: *An advertisement for the opening of the Alhambra Bar, Hill Street.*

Left: *The Crown Inn, at the junction of Hill Street and Station Street.*

Just the other side of Severn Street is the Bright House, an M&B pub, taking its name from the nearby John Bright Street. The house began life as the 1960s Glue Pot. Why it was so named was always a bit of a mystery. Looking a little stale by the 1970s, it was closed down and totally refurbished. The house reopened as Sam Weller's in July 1979. The name comes from a character in Charles Dicken's *Pickwick Papers*. In September 2005 the pub's name was changed to the Bright House. This 1960s triangular block in which Bright's is situated was built to replace a Blitzed site. Before the war M&B had another public pub on this site, the Malt Shovel at 88 Hill Street. An early Victorian house, it was updated by architect R.J. Matthews in 1884. In 1899, M&B bought the house, and brought in James & Lister Lea to design an extension. They submitted plans on 31 May 1899 for a semi-circular structure to Matthews' house. More than twenty years after the end of the war, M&B submitted plans for the development of this large corner block. The result was the Savoy Hotel, and a new public house, the Alhambra. The décor of the house was Victorian, many of the original features had been saved after the closure of the old Woodman in Easy Row. The pub was on two levels, with a second entrance around the corner in John Bright Street. Losing popularity its name changed to the Parasol.

Three houses in Hill Street still remain. The Spread Eagle, a beerhouse, appears in the obituary of its former owner, 'Mrs Higson', in the 21 November 1821 edition of the *Birmingham Gazette*. The Rose & Crown at 1 Hill Street, on the corner of New Inkleys, originated post-1818. The first known licensee was John Harbidge, who died in August 1829. The Rose & Crown closed in 1856 for the building of New Street Station. The last of the public houses in Hill Street is the existing Crown Hotel, on the corner of Station Street. It is first listed in Kelly's Directory of Birmingham for 1896. The Crown was a William Butler's tied house, allegedly designed by Birmingham architect Thomas Plevins. The house still retains much of its original features, including its long public bar, and an original large M&B mirror. The first licensee of the Crown was John Webb, landlord for over twenty years. In 1996 it gathered the Dutch overspill from Raphael's, as Dutch, Scots and Swiss football supporters watched their teams on the big TV screens, and played pool against the natives. It was a good time.

Back outside again, and left down to Smallbrook Street; this survey of the Bull Ring and Inner Ring Road pubs is now complete. In the course of this survey over 760 individual pubs have been recorded. A second volume on Central Birmingham pubs is in preparation and will cover the remaining central Birmingham area limited by the Middle Ring Road.

INDEX

Brickmakers' Arms, Thomas Street 72
Bright House, Hill Street 154
Britannia, Princip Street 60
British Oak, Suffolk Street 142
Brown Derby, Colmore Circus 98
Brown Lion, Dale End 36
Brown Lion, Snow Hill 46
Bull, Bull Street 43
Bull Ring Tavern, St Martin's Lane 25
Bullivant's Hotel, High Street 33
Bull's Head, Dale End 36
Bull's Head, Dudley Street 135
Bull's Head, Hill Street 151
Bull's Head, Lichfield Street 68
Bull's Head, Minories 44
Bull's Head, Moor Street 66
Bull's Head, Old Inkleys 134
Bull's Head, Pinfold Street 145
Bull's Head, Price Street 59-60
Bull's Head, Smallbrook Street 136
Bull's Head, Stafford Street 62
Bull's Head, Upper Priory 74
Bull's Head, Whittall Street 57
Bull's Head Liquor Vaults, Smallbrook St 136
Burlington Hotel, New Street 136
Bushwackers, Edmund Street 104
Butcher's Arms, Bell Street 130
Byron's Head, Newhall Street 108

Cabin, Dale End 43
Cabin, Old Square 43, 73
Cabin, Union Passage 123
Cagney's, Cannon Street 89
Cannon, Cannon Street 89
Canterbury Tavern, Bull Ring 21
Carpe Diem, Great Charles Street 105
Carriers' Arms, Moor Street 66
Castle, Steelhouse Lane 55-56
Castle, Suffolk Street 142
Castle Inn, High Street 32-33
Castle Punchbowl, Steelhouse Lane 55
Castle Vaults, High Street 33
Castle & Falcon, Snow Hill 48
Cathedral, Weaman Street 57
Cathedral Tavern, Church Street 110
Chain, Bull Street 46
Chain, Edgbaston Street 129
Chapel Tavern, Great Charles Street 107
Chapel Tavern, Whittall Street 57-59
Chequer, Suffolk Street 142
Chequers, Snow Hill, 48
Chequers, Steelhouse Lane 52
Church Tavern, Church Street 109
Circo Bar, Suffolk Street 142

Clarendon Vaults, Temple Street 91
Clements, High Street 35
Coach & Horses, Dale End 36
Coach & Horses, Bell Street, 130
Coach & Horses, Edgbaston Street 124
Coach & Horses, Lichfield Street 68
Coach & Horses, Market Street 105
Coach & Horses, New Meeting Street 35-36
Coach & Horses, Pinfold Street 145
Coach & Horses, Snow Hill 48
Coach & Horses, Steelhouse Lane 55
Coach & Horses, Whittall Street 57
Coach & Horses, Worcester Street 131
Coachsmith's Arms, Loveday Street 60
Coal Hole, Needless Alley 89
Cock Inn, Bull Ring 20
Cock Inn, Lichfield Street 68
Cock Inn, Steelhouse Lane 52
Coffee House, Bell Street 129
Coffee Pot, Cherry Street 121
Coffee Pot, Dale End 37
Coffee Tavern, Bull Street 45
Cold Bath, Loveday Street 60
Colmore Hotel, Church Street 110
Colmore Inn, Church Street 110
Colmore Rest, Church Street 110
Comet, High Street 17
Commercial Hotel, New Street 78
Continental, Moor Street 67
Cooke's Tavern, Cherry Orchard 121
Corn Exchange Vaults, High Street 33
Corn Market, Bell Street 130
Corner, Moor Street 66
Corner Cupboard, Union Passage 122
Corner House, Edmund Street 104
Corner Luncheon Stores, Union Passage 122
Costermonger, Dalton Way 61
Country Girl, Navigation Street 147
Crispin, High Street 36
Crispin, New Street 89
Crispin, Paradise Street 142
Criterion, Suffolk Street 140
Cross, Smallbrook Street 140
Cross Guns, Dale End 42-43
Cross Pistols, Slaney Street 59
Crown, Cherry Street 121

Crown, Corporation Street 71
Crown, Edmund Street 104
Crown, High Street 36
Crown, Hill Street 154
Crown (Old), John Street 73
Crown, Moor Street 66
Crown, Newton Street 73
Crown, Old Meeting Street 134
Crown, Smallbrook Street 140
Crown, Snow Hill 25
Crown, Thomas Street 73
Crown & Anchor, Livery Street 113
Crown & Pensioner, Moor Street 66
Crystal Palace, Smallbrook Street 140
Cup, Lichfield Street 68
Cup, Moor Street 66
Cutlers' Arms, John Street 73

Dee's Hotel, Temple Row 91
Derby House, Hill Street 151
Diamond, Anthony 17, 57
Digress, Newhall Street 108
Dingley's Hotel, Moor Street 66
Dog, Loveday Street 60
Dog, New Inkleys 134
Dog, Spiceal Street 15
Dog & Doublet, Weaman Street 57
Dog & Duck, Edmund Street 102
Dog & Magpie, Slaney Street 59
Dog & Partridge, Loveday Street 60
Dolphin, Bull Ring 11-12
Dolphin, Monmouth Street 98
Dolphin, Steelhouse Lane 52
Dolphin (Old), Suffolk Street 142
Druid's Head, Edmund Street 104
Dublin Tavern, Little Charles Street 100
Dun Cow, Pinfold Street 145

Eagle & Ball, Colmore Street 132
Eagle & Child, Smallbrook Street 139
Eagle & Child, Whittall Street 57
Edmunds, Robert 146
Elephant & Castle, Pinfold Street 145
Empire Vaults, Smallbrook Street 140
Engine Inn, (Old), Dale End 36-37
Era, Smallbrook Street 140
Exchange, Stephenson Street 135

Factotem & Firkin, Bennett's Hill 91
Falcon, Edgbaston Street 129
Falcon, Newhall Street 109
Falstaff, Bull Street 44

Street 135
Southall, John 45, 146
Sportsman, Lichfield Street 68
Sportsman, Worcester Street 131
Spread Eagle, Hill Street 154
Spread Eagle, Spiceal Street 17
Sputnik, Temple Street 92
Square Peg, Corporation Street 71
Stag's Head, Navigation Street 146
Stag's Head, Stafford Street 62
Stage, Paradise Place 145
Stamp, Steelhouse Lane 52
Star, Dudley Street 135
Star, High Street 31
Star, Lichfield Street 69
Star & Bull's Head, Dale End 36
Star & Garter, Hill Street 151
Star Wine Vaults, Dale End 43
State Cabin, Dale End 43
Station Bar, New Street Station 135
Steam Coach Tavern, Newton
  Street 73
Stevens Bar, High Street 27
Stone Cross, Dale End 37
Stores, Lower Priory 73
Stores, Smallbrook Street 136
Stork, Old Square 73
Stour Valley Hotel, Union Passage
  122
Struggler Alive, Moor Street 66
Styles Hotel, Temple Row 91
Suffield's Bar, Union Passage 122
Sultan's Divan, Needless Alley 89
Sun, Worcester Street 131
Swan, Bull Street 45
Swan, Dale End 41
Swan, High Street 13, 27
Swan, Lichfield Street 68
Swan Hotel, New Street 78
Swan & Railway, Hill Street 151
Swan Luncheon Bar, Navigation
  Street 147
Swan with Two Necks, Livery
  Street 110
Swan with Two Necks, St Martin's
  Lane 23
Sydenham, Edgbaston Street 124

Tainsh's Hotel, Old Square 73
Talbot, New Inkley's 134
Talbot, Spiceal Street 15
Tamworth Arms, Moor Street 62
Taurus Bar, New Street Station 135
Tavern in the Town, New Street
  84
Taylor's, Cherry Street 122
Teddy's, New Street 84
Temple Bar, Temple Street 92, 94
Theatre, Hill Street 151
Theatre, Smallbrook Street 140

Three Crowns, Steelhouse Lane 55
Three Crowns, Suffolk Street 142
Three Crowns, Worcester Street
  131
Three Horse Shoes, St. Martin's
  Lane 23
Three Tuns, Livery Street 111
Three Tuns, Pinfold Street 146
Three Tuns, Smallbrook Street 140
Three Tuns, Snow Hill 48
Three Tuns, Thomas Street 72
Tiger, Church Street 109
Tonk's Hotel, Hill Street 151
Toreador, Edgbaston Street 129
Town Hall Stores, New Street 82
Town Hall Tavern, Ann Street 98
Trocadero, Temple Street 92
Turk's Head, Bath Street 59
Turk's Head, Bell Street 130
Turk's Head, Carrs Lane 35
Turk's Head, Edgbaston Street 124
Turk's Head, Lichfield Street 68
Turk's Head, Livery Street 113
Turk's Head, Steelhouse Lane 55
Turk's Head, Worcester Street 131
Turtle, Bull Street 46

Unicorn, Bell Street 130
Unicorn, Hill Street 151
Union Bar, Union Street 122
Union Inn, Union Street 122-3

Victoria, John Bright Street 149
Victoria, Stafford Street 62
Victoria Arms, Steelhouse Lane 55
Victoria's, Hill Street 149
Viking, Smallbrook Queensway
  140
Vine, Navigation Street 147
Vine, Snow Hill 46-47

Waggon & Horses, Dale End 42
Waggon & Horses, Edgbaston
  Street 124
Waggon & Horses, Edmund Street
  104
Waggon & Horses, Livery Street
  110
Wandering Minstrel, Bull Ring 25,
  66, 140
Warwick Arms, Snow Hill 50
Watchmakers Arms, Edmund
  Street 104
Waterloo Bar, New Street 80, 82
Waterloo Tavern, Lower Priory 73
Waterloo Tavern, Moor Street 67
Weatherspoon's, Paradise Forum
  145
Wein Keller, Edmund Street 100
Welch Harper, Bath Street 59

Wellington, Bennett's Hill 89-90
West End Bar, Snow Hill 52
Westwood, John 69, 120
Westwood, Tom 69, 120
Wheatsheaf, Bull Ring 17
Wheatsheaf, New Street, 74, 78
Wheatsheaf, Suffolk Street 140
Wheel, Snow Hill 51
White Hart, Church Street 109
White Hart, Colmore Row 98
White Hart, Paradise Street 145
White Horse, Bull Ring 13
White Horse, Congreve Street 115
White Horse, Livery Street 111
White Horse, Moor Stree 66
White Horse, Steelhouse Lane 52
White House, Whittall Street 59
White Lion, Ann Street 98
White Lion, Bell Street 122
White Lion, Lichfield Street 69
White Lion, Moor Street 64
White Lion, Navigation Street 147
White Lion, Snow Hill 46
White Swan, Church Street 109
White Swan, Edmund Street 104,
  110
White Swan, Moor Street 67
White Swan, Navigation Street
  146
White Swan, Phillips Street 131
White Swan, Smallbrook Street 136
White Swan, Snow Hill 51-52
White Swan, Temple Row 91
White Swan, Thomas Street 72
White Swan, Upper Priory 74
White Swan, Weaman Street 57
Windsor, Cannon Street 89
Wine & Spirit Stores, Bull Street
  45
Wine & Spirit Stores, Dale End 37
Wine & Spirit Stores, High Street
  36
Wine & Spirit Stores, Snow Hill
  51
Wine & Spirit Vaults, Worcester
  Street 131
Woodman, Ann Street 98
Woodman, Easy Row 23, 69, 120-
  1, 132, 154
Woolpack, Moor Street 62-64
Woolpack, Spiceal Street 15, 23-24
Wyldicatte, High Street 28

Yard of Ale, New Street 84
Yates' Wine Lodge, Corporation
  Street 71
York Hotel, Edgbaston Street 129